"G. F. Watkins has resolved a critical problem with an original solution to build our churches by keeping and discipling converts who would otherwise be lost. To these issues faced by every leader, G.F. Watkins gives a Biblically-based answer which I applaud."

— Doug Stringer, Somebody Cares America, and Turning Point Ministries International

"The Holy Spirit has taken another step in bringing men into their rightful place with Him, both in the family and in the Church. I highly recommend this work done by G.F. to every man who has come to know Jesus as Savior and Lord."

— Dr. Hilton Sutton Th.D.

"Closing the back door is what the G-MEN strategy is all about. Pastor G. F. Watkins is a man whom God has raised up to help pastors around the world close the back door and retain the harvest. This strategy will not only close the door but raise up a new generation of leaders through its powerful mentoring program. This is not just a theory, but is evident through his life and ministry. It's awesome what God has done through Pastor Watkins in just a few short years. I highly recommend this and encourage pastors that if you have been praying for something to close the back door to your church—LOOK NO FURTHER. Strong Men—Strong Leaders—Strong Homes—Strong Churches."

— Rodney M. Howard-Browne Th.D, D.Min, DD, Founding Pastor, The River, Tampa Bay

G-MEN: THE FINAL STRATEGY

Together We Win!

by G. F. Watkins

watercolor books™

Southlake, Texas

G-MEN: The Final Strategy
Together We Win!

ISBN: 1-931682-00-3
Copyright © 2001 by G. F. Watkins
PowerHouse Christian Center
1818 Katyland Drive
Katy, TX 77493

Published by Watercolor Books™
P. O. Box 93234
Southlake, TX 76092-3234
www.watercolorbooks.com

Unless otherwise indicated, all Scripture quotations are taken
from the *King James Version* of the Bible.

Scripture quotations marked (NIV) are taken from the *Holy
Bible, New International Version* ®. NIV ® Copyright © 1973,
1978, 1984 by International Bible Society. Used by permission
of Zondervan Publishing House. All rights reserved.

To Rose

ACKNOWLEDGEMENTS

Thanks to my wife, Rose, for allowing God to use her as an illustrated sermon to teach me about how He sees His Church. And for her support in this and many other projects in my life!

Thanks to my sons for showing me how to be a better father.

Thanks to my mother, Gwen Watkins, for praying for me and believing that I would come to know Jesus when I was not saved.

Thanks to my father, Gayle Watkins, for teaching me what it's like to be a person of character and integrity.

Thanks to Dr. Edwin Louis Cole for writing *Maximized Manhood* and for being a spiritual father to me. I am so grateful for the times he has spoken into my life, believed in me, molded me, exhorted and encouraged me.

Thanks to Pastor Walter Hallam for hiring me out of my secular coaching job and showing me what it is like to be a minister. I feel like he birthed me into the ministry.

Thanks to the men and women of PowerHouse Christian Center for allowing me to be their pastor. God has called people from all over the world to co-labor together at PHCC and I am so grateful that He has put me in this strategic area to raise up end-time warriors!

TABLE OF CONTENTS

FOREWORD

This is a book that challenges reality as it tells the truth. Truth is the foundation for good and godly character. All truth is confrontational. Truth demands change. Change creates crisis. Crisis causes change.

This is a book written by a man who loves truth. His success resulted from teaching and practicing truth. He is a man who does not practice what he preaches, but preaches what he practices.

One of his friends said, *"When opportunity appears, it is spelled W-O-R-K. Most people do not take advantage of opportunity, or are indifferent to it, because they don't want more work."*

More work requires more commitment. Commitment requires the giving of self—living outside the "comfort zone" on the edge. But when all is said and done, the edge is the safest place because it's where God lives. That is enough of a reason to read this book, find the wealth of truth, and begin to do what it teaches.

G. F. Watkins is a doer, not a talker. This is a book for people who want to challenge their perceptions of reality, escape to a life of real truth, walk on the edge, excel in character, become superior in mentoring, and achieve a Christlike quality of leadership that is rich and rewarding.

Dreaming without doing is foolishness, the proverb reads—so is reading without doing. This is a book for doers who read. Thank you, G. F., for being a doer, for studying, practicing, writing and challenging us today with this new strategy.

Edwin Louis Cole
Founder and President
Christian Men's Network

Introduction

"And they sang together by course in praising and giving thanks unto the Lord; because he is good, for his mercy endureth forever toward Israel. And all the people shouted with a great shout, when they praised the Lord, because the foundation of the house of the Lord was laid.

"But many of the priests and Levites and chief of the fathers, who were ancient men, that had seen the first house, when the foundation of this house was laid before their eyes, wept with a loud voice; and many shouted aloud for joy."[1]

The foundation was laid, and the people rejoiced. The ancient men who had seen the first House wept and shouted because they realized the return of the glory of God was at hand. One of the first indications of the effect of the strategy you're about to read was the response from "God's generals," people who had seen the crusades of the 40's and 50's that had exponentially increased the Kingdom. They became encouraged, excited as they saw the G-MEN strategy as building the House of God. Having experienced the glory of God's presence in their lifetime, they recognized the return to an even great revival.

"The glory of this latter house shall be greater than of the former, saith the Lord of hosts."[2]

The House will be greater today because it's being built on principles of integrity and enthusiasm, not emotions or a pep rally. Hype is not needed when we go out and work in the harvest fields of salvation as our lives were intended.

It's been said, "We are all the same age, just deposited on earth to accomplish our purpose in His Plan—to win back the man!"

We are eternal beings. God knew us in our mother's wombs. He placed us strategically on this planet for this specific time to facilitate His divine plan. In all of Heaven or Hell, we will forever be known as one who did, or did not, fulfill His purpose in the hour He gave us.

In my football coaching days, I'd say, "Let the game begin!"

Remember—God made us to win!

"Now thanks be unto God, which always causeth us to triumph in Christ, and maketh manifest the savour of his knowledge by us in every place."[3]

[1] Ezra 3:11-12
[2] Haggai 2:9
[3] II Corinthians 2:14

A New Strategy

Floods rose and the city cracked under the crushing pressure of tons of water. In one dark, soaked weekend, Houston's infrastructure of roads, buildings and drains gave way to disaster, leaving hundreds homeless and billions of dollars in damage.

Days later, Dan's stomach turned to knots as he drove through the neighborhood he'd called "home" as a boy. Filled with crack dealers, the impoverished inhabitants and drug users only scraped by, even without a federal emergency aggravating their lives. Now they were starving, hurting, devastated. Heartbroken and feeling helpless, Dan turned his car toward home.

That weekend he mentioned the plight of this neighborhood during a home group meeting.

"Let's go help them!" the leader said.

Working fast, the group put together fifty sacks of groceries before heading out for the site. On their arrival, they found other churches already delivering food and water, so Dan's home group joined them. As they worked, Dan's group started telling people about the Gospel. One man claimed he was 78 years old, and that he'd lived a life of crime.

"Where would you have gone if you had died in the flood, Sir?" asked Dan's wife, Denise.

The man jerked his thumb to point down and said, "Straight to hell."

"You don't need to go there!" Denise said. Then she spelled out the plan of salvation from Scripture and prayed with the man to receive Christ.

Another older woman claimed she'd been the mistress of a mobster, and had been living in hiding ever since to protect herself. Now suffering from Parkinson's disease, she was eager to hear about Jesus the Healer. By the time the group had finished ministering to her, she was saved and praying for healing.

Fifty bags of food didn't look like enough, but between all the churches' efforts, by day's end, every person with a need had received an answer to their need, and 27 people had given their lives to Christ.

That scene of a little group pulling together, addressing a situation, and evangelizing is happening over and over because of something I call the "G-MEN" strategy. Birthed from an intense need, inspired by the pain of helplessness, the strategy now set in motion is operating, producing fruit for the kingdom of God day in and day out.

A little over two years before that Houston flood, I lay in the sun on a beautiful beach pondering the most serious problem I'd faced in pastoring our rapidly-growing church. Any pastor might have been happy with hundreds added to church membership each year. But my congregation was filled with go-getters, real soul-winners, and they were bringing thousands to Christ annually. So why was our membership only growing by hundreds?

Like a flood, people were surging in, then surging right out the back door into oblivion. We expended large amounts of time, energy and money to bring in new families, but they whooshed out the back door once they received one answer from God.

I could not stop thinking about the ones we lost, who were saved but never really healed or delivered, who never joined our membership nor found their place in the Body of

Christ overall. I had accepted the pastoral call to shepherd a flock, but now I was forced to watch helplessly as, one by one, sheep ventured into the world unprepared, likely to become prey for the enemy.

I was tired of working to *obtain* souls with no structure, strategy or plan to *maintain* the people, the fruit of our labors. Like the great shepherd-boy David from Bible days, I was discontent with sitting and watching. Whether it involved killing a bear or lion, as it had for him, I was going to find a way to protect these sheep God had entrusted to me. This could not, would not, happen to my flock—not on my watch!

One of the books I'd taken on vacation was about the G-12 cell church strategy by Joel Comisky. I wanted to learn all I could about cell churches, as they seemed to be the fastest-growing churches on earth. Nineteen of the twenty largest churches in the world are cell churches!

We had created *home groups*, after David Yonggi Cho's model from Seoul, South Korea, with moderate success. The constant cycle to raise "baby Christians," then turn around and start all over again, left our home group leaders unfulfilled. Even as natural parents, we don't mind the effort and sacrifice to raise our children. But when the grandbabies come, we don't want to start over. We want to hold them, love them, play with them, then give them back when it's time to feed and change them!

Our home group leaders were pouring into people, praying with them, counseling and discipling their group members so they could handle running a group of their own eventually. The problem was, those converts matured and began their own cell groups, so the leaders had to start again with new believers.

God had directed me toward the "cell church" structure. Relationships are crucial to plant people in the church and the Body of Christ. And the cell group model promotes and cultivates relationships. But there was a *missing link*, a key ingredient, keeping it from functioning with ease to its maximum effect.

I came home from vacation still perplexed and troubled in my spirit. The next weekend, I attended the "Lion's Roar" International Men's Event in Fort Worth, Texas, hosted by Dr. Edwin Louis Cole and the Christian Men's Network. Sitting in a leaders' meeting, my answer suddenly rose up within my spirit. I realized what I'd known for years and had just read again—*Jesus preached to the multitudes, but He discipled and mentored only twelve!*

Now Dr. Cole was talking about mentoring men. It hit me that I could teach and disciple twelve men to do what I had done, perhaps even better than I'd done, then ask them to do the same with others. What if I developed a life-long mentoring relationship with twelve home group leaders and they mentored twelve home group leaders themselves? The home groups could multiply without dividing, and each man could pour himself into *one* generation of disciples. We could progress past "babies" and birth "grandbabies" in the same way we do in the physical realm, through our "sons."

Already, of the successful and powerful ministries I knew here in the U.S., all were built on the strength of men's ministry—charging men to take responsibility for the spiritual condition of the home, church and community. Bishop Eddie Long, for example, spent every Saturday discipling and maturing the men in his church and his church grew to over 20,000 members. Pastors Art Sepulveda in Hawaii, Kong Hee in Singapore, Tom Deuschle in Zimbabwe, James Meeks in Chicago, all took CMN teachings on manhood and raised up powerful ministries by raising up powerful men.

What if I combined the emphasis on men with the idea of the cell church and started "majoring in men" in ministry, while taking care of the needs and concerns of the women and children at the same time through those very same men! What if we built relationships between men on a regular basis, not in an awkward "accountability group" or a monthly breakfast where men could hide behind smiles while flipping flapjacks!

Sitting in that CMN leadership meeting, my mind wandered back to Joel Comisky's book on the G-12 concept, where every leader is responsible for discipling twelve, who then become leaders who are responsible to disciple twelve more. I was being challenged merely to do what Moses had been instructed by his father-in-law, Jethro. I was copying what Jesus did in order to build His Church. I picked up a pen and wrote some notes to myself.

Those notes indirectly resulted in a man mobilizing an entire group with ease to meet the need for charity and evangelism in a neighborhood after a flood. The pastor didn't have to give a special stamp of approval. The "evangelism" committee didn't have to meet with the "hospitality" committee to make it happen. The group simply mobilized like a SWAT team, bringing a spiritually-alert answer to a desperate need.

The Body of Christ has recognized the need for men to take an active role of leadership. Perhaps more than in any previous generation, the role of Biblical manhood is being preached today. Men as leader-servants, lovers of truth, stewards of our communities and resources, and lovers of our wives and children. Ministers all over the world are challenging men to love their wives as Christ loves the Church.

CMN teaches men that *manhood and Christlikeness are synonymous*. In a previous decade, that revelation changed my life and marriage, and propelled me into the role of a pastor. I had such a conviction to teach men about God's instructions for achieving victory in life that the first development of my ministry gifts came from teaching Dr. Cole's book, *Maximized Manhood*.

I had started ministering wherever anyone would listen—in jails, schools, churches and even in casual settings with my friends and loved ones. It seemed as if every time I spoke, the revelation of Biblical manhood set men free and gave them a sense of purpose.

For that reason, since the very first meeting of "PowerHouse" Christian Center, I have taught that God called *men* to lead as kings and priests in this world. As a result, men embraced the truth and simplicity of God's plan for their marriages, and hundreds of couples were spared the pain of abuse, neglect and divorce. While the message of maximized manhood is *about* men, it is *for* women because when a man becomes more Christlike, he nourishes, cherishes and admonishes others, including his wife and children, to exercise their own gifts and callings.

Now that same message, being Christlike, was producing a shift in my thinking, a refocusing and honing in on the direction God was revealing. As a leader, I needed to become more Christlike by mentoring twelve as Christ had done, and the entire church would benefit. But it had to start with me. As the pastor, I had to pour myself into twelve men and form relationships that would allow me to speak truth into their lives. That would take commitment on their part, and mine.

I made my notes, then set them aside to hear the rest of the meeting, knowing in my heart that many hours of prayer and fasting were ahead of me. I couldn't speak the vision until I had a plan so easy to duplicate, the mentoring process could be reproduced by my men, and then their men, and so on.

It was like old Texas football. I'd been a high school football coach, and I'd expected to win—not by fancy or "trick" plays, but by mastering a basic, simple plan that could win ballgames. In Texas we were once famous for our wishbone offense. It's nothing fancy, nothing new, but we learned it and practiced it until we perfected it. With that wishbone offense, we'd take high school teams out on the field and win game after game after game.

That's what I was doing now. Sorting through important details like who to draft onto my initial team, when to meet, what to study and how to ensure the success of this mentoring program. I did not want to burn out an already burnt-out generation. I just wanted to see the fire of God take hold in a man's life! For that, I needed a simple plan. Something we could execute. Something we practice, perfect, then duplicate again and again and again.

After months of prayer and preparation, the G-MEN strategy was ready to launch. "G-MEN" is the old term for FBI agents that I resurrected to stand for "God's Men." We are His agents in this earth, His "hit men," His team, His G-MEN.

G-MEN would be godly men, men with the nature of God in them. G-MEN would form governments of twelve to act as spiritual "Special Forces," sent to bring truth, healing and restoration to a dying world. G-MEN would be leaders in the move of God, using their gifts and talents to build God's Kingdom. G-MEN would become loving husbands who treated their wives as joint-heirs. Their children would understand the love of the Father through their example.

G-MEN would be bold warriors in God's army, not hesitating to invade the enemy's camp to bring light into darkness. G-MEN would exemplify the nature and character of Christ, provoking other men to join the fight for the souls of humanity. G-MEN would become the *missing link* for our church, and The Church!

As I'd prayed while developing the strategy, I felt the Lord say I'd do more than watch G-MEN grow our church. He told me through His Word to write the vision and make it plain—so plain that any leader who wanted to close the back door of the church could run this plan and win!

It's the G-MEN *strategy*. It connects the *problem* with a *plan*. It is mapped out step by step, to work for any leader, any group, any culture, anywhere in the world. The local church is God's vehicle for *revival*. To drive the vehicle, we don't need to reinvent the wheel. We just need to fix a couple of spokes!

In the first year of the G-MEN strategy, our church attendance increased almost 50%. We grew from the original ten men whom I felt God had told me to choose, into one hundred and fifty men in just a year, multiplying my efforts fifteen times without multiplying my energies or time. People like Dan and Denise plugged into the vision and committed themselves to the church.

Our next goal is 1500 men. And the next is 15,000 men and their families on board. Imagine what God can accomplish when that many families are faithful to the church, committed to the vision and willing to labor together in the harvest fields!

Through the G-MEN strategy, even unstable church members become stable and then are equipped and able to participate in the ministry of reconciliation and fulfill the Great Commission. God's commanded blessing has been activated and we're experiencing an outpouring of His miracle-working power on a consistent basis. We've now developed discipleship tools that make it easy to walk new converts through the spiritual maturation process. This has created a true army of God and increased our church's capability to accomplish the vision.

People have exposed, postulated about, written up, and tried to close the "back door" problem of converts leaving the church for decades. By keeping our eyes and ears open to what God is doing around the world, and our hearts in tune with Him, we have developed practical applications to bring order, build the church, and take the Gospel to the world. It's no longer theory for us. It's a time-tested plan of action that is producing supernatural results. It's a world-changing revelation for this end-time generation — a final strategy!

Anyone who wants to duplicate their ministry by working smarter, not harder, can benefit. Whether it's youth ministry, food bank ministry, or evangelism outreach, this is a leadership strategy that works!

Taking a look at Christian history, we can see a relay race of sorts. God's plan is for one generation to hand off to another all that had been entrusted to them. Have we done all we can with what was handed to us? Will we pass to our "spiritual sons" something even more than what we were handed?

The G-MEN strategy is a *tool* for building men and raising up sons. The reconciliation process that G-MEN so effectively brings to the world will carry on long after we are gone, leaving an inheritance for our children's children. Can the G-MEN strategy change the world? It already is! Pastors from nations all over the world are embracing this strategy and equipping their churches to reach their regions as never before.

2

THE NEED FOR PURPOSE

John and Tammy were filled with tremendous potential, but lacked for direction. As a result, their home was divided. Like so many good people, they had been in church but hadn't found God's purpose for their lives. John and Tammy wanted to do right, but needed guidance, instruction and relationships to move them toward a significant destination.

My wife Rose and I had already experienced challenges in ministering to hurting people, so we sought God for wisdom about this couple. I felt the Lord's gentle nudge to take John and Tammy under our wings—up close.

John allowed me to speak straight to him, and even correct him. I told him the buck stopped with him. He could no longer blame Tammy, the in-laws or the church for what went on in his home. If he was to be reconciled to his wife and children, he had to accept responsibility.

The Bible promises that God will give a man wisdom to "dwell accordingly" with his wife.[1] God has promised it. It's our responsibility to ask for and receive His wisdom to live in peace in our homes. John came to realize that every answer he needed for his marriage was in the Word of God. Through prayer, wisdom would overcome every bit of confusion.

For six months, Rose and I spoke with John and Tammy every day—sometimes more than once a day. When John would mess up, Tammy would call Rose. When Tammy would mess up, John would call me. Rose and I worked as a team to help stabilize their marriage.

People in desperate situations often try escaping by seeking out others who are just as desperate. That's insane! When we fall into the wells of life, we don't need advice from people in the same well. We need someone who is out of the well to throw us a rope and help us climb out.

THEIR OWN WORDS

John and Tammy submitted to mentoring, and everything in their lives changed. But I can do better than tell you about them. I'll give them the floor to tell you in their own words:

Tammy

That which is impossible with men is possible with God. Our marriage was beyond restoration. It had to be resurrected, and God did perform the impossible. But God also knows that you can't maintain a loving healthy marriage with an old mindset so He provided a way to renew our minds through mentoring. I have seen my husband mature, not because three years have passed, but because mentoring is such an effective discipleship tool. When I started to see my husband change, my natural reaction was to want to change myself.

John

Tammy and I had been married for seven years when she told me she wanted to separate. I didn't understand why. I was working, I helped around the house, didn't drink, party or fool around. I knew we had arguments and things weren't the best, but things weren't that bad—to me.

Tammy's desire to separate was a wake-up call. We agreed to counseling, and Tammy made a list of all my problems— "not a nice person, mean to people, controlling, demand-

ing, bad temper." I decided I would do whatever it took to change my life and win my wife's love back.

Pastor Watkins began to mentor me. He said if I would do as he said, Tammy would have the husband she always wanted and I would have the wife I always wanted. I didn't believe that, but wanted my wife back enough to try. As I began to listen and act on the principles he taught me, I noticed changes in my life that drew me closer to God and drew my wife closer to me.

One incident in particular changed the way I treated my wife forever. Tammy got real mad one day and said there was no way she would ever love me again. She was dead serious. I accepted it and drove around in the car to clear my head.

I called Pastor and explained the situation. He asked if I thought it was permanent. I said yes. He asked if I believed in healing. I said I did. He asked if God could heal cancer. I said He could. He asked me why. I said the Word promised healing and I had seen a few people healed before. Then I began to understand that God could heal my marriage, no matter what, because God can raise up something dead and bring it back to life.

*From that time forward, I never doubted again God's power in our lives. Rapid change ensued. I changed from an introvert to an extrovert. I began to make friends. I courted my wife until I won back her love. Now I believe we have one of the best marriages in the world. Every Saturday, we sit down and study together. Also, I mentor a group of men and my wife mentors their wives. God is **good**.*

Modeling a healthy, happy marriage for John and Tammy was my first experience at mentoring. The dramatic change in them made me a believer in the mentoring process.

Scripture teaches that when we are forgiven for much, we love much.[2] In John and Tammy's hearts, that happened. The problem wasn't getting them inside a church. It was getting the church inside them! They needed mentors to help rub the Word of God into their hearts until they could apply Biblical principles on their own.

A lesson was ingrained in me after mentoring John and Tammy. Preaching by itself isn't sufficient for significant success in people's lives. Preaching can create converts. But Christ told us to make *disciples*. Mentoring is the answer.

Now, how to do it? Where to start?

"Without a vision the people perish."[3] At first, John had no idea what his purpose was in his family. John and Tammy had no vision of where they were going or what they could accomplish. That's typical today. We don't know *why* we exist or *why* we need to change. And when we don't know *why*, we feel like *"Why bother?"*

The word "purpose" is defined, "The object for which something exists or is done; intention; aim."[4]

People ask, *"Who am I and what is my purpose for living?"* Without a sense of purpose we live unfulfilled and often depressed lives. Without purpose for faith and spirituality, even Christians become discouraged. Most Christians at first get saved to avoid hell. We get "fire insurance" and then struggle through life until God calls us home.

There is more to being a Christian than dying and going to Heaven! There is purpose between the born-again experience and our eternal rest.

JESUS' PURPOSE

"For this purpose the Son of God was manifested, that he might destroy the works of the devil."[5] To comprehend this, we have to understand that the devil's works include sickness, strife and poverty—but those are just symptoms. His original work came from the original sin.

God commanded Adam to dress, serve, labor and work, and to keep, protect and preserve the Garden of Eden.[6] Before Eve was ever created, God held Adam accountable to supervise and govern the garden. Then came the devil in the form of a serpent.[7] According to God's commanded order, the devil had to submit to Adam and Eve. The devil had to *ask* Eve to eat the fruit! She had authority over him. But the devil deceived humanity, Eve submitted to Satan, Adam failed in leadership and God's order was literally turned upside down.

We see God's order reversed in homes across America and the world, where the devil has control over the home. The children manipulate the parents through rebellion. The wife or mother tries to take a stand and fix the household. The man is apathetic, blames his wife and avoids accountability. That's the "works of the devil" Jesus came to destroy!

Satan's works are not just a few particular evils, such as murder or adultery. His work is perverting and reversing the order God intended. The Garden was God's plan for humanity. It was a place of divine order, which always equates to peace, protection and freedom.

Jesus intended to put us back into God's original order. He taught us to walk in authority over the devil, to take responsibility and accountability for the condition of the world around us. *Jesus reversed the curse that Adam caused.*

"For as by one man's disobedience many were made sinners, so by the obedience of one shall many be made righteous."[8] Jesus did His part to put the devil back in submission. Now we have to do our part to restore men, in particular, back to their place of authority over him.

Since we have Adam's nature in us, it does not come naturally to flow in God's order. Human beings do not like to submit. We must be born again with the Spirit of God and nature of Christ inside us if we are to submit to God's plan and overcome the flesh and the devil. Jesus said, "Not my will, but thy will, Father," which was the greatest act of submission mankind has ever known.[9]

We must be born again to see God's divine order and blessings manifest in our lives. Getting saved is the most important decision we'll ever make. Yet it's just the first step to fulfilling our destiny as a Christian.

THE BELIEVER'S PURPOSE

In our quest for purpose, we often seek happiness and fulfillment in our spouse, children, money, career or other temporal things. However, as Christians, our purpose for living no longer revolves around earthly circumstances. We have something far more important in our lives.

God has given us an eternal purpose beyond natural relationships or accomplishments. The purpose for every born-again believer is found in the words, "Go ye into all the world and preach the gospel to every creature."[10] Our purpose, our calling, our reason for living is to win souls for the Kingdom of God. Our fulfilment comes when we destroy the works of the enemy and accomplish God's plan—to bring humanity back to His Garden.

If we just attend church to learn how to be "better Christians," we've missed it! Christians are not "better people," we're soul winners! Certainly being a Christian makes us a better spouse and parent, but if we ever stop winning souls, we've missed our purpose. As believers, we must ask ourselves, "What am I doing to fulfill my purpose?"

The Church's Purpose

The only way to become more efficient and successful at winning souls is by corporate effort. The local church is the strategy house where Christians are mobilized to take the Gospel to the world. A church with purpose will give its members an outlet to live out their purpose. We must learn how to win souls in the fields, then bring the new converts to church. This is how we build the army of God and become a greater force against the kingdom of darkness.

As I see it in Scripture, churches have a three-fold purpose: *win, disciple* and *send.*

Win

In our fourth year of existence as a church, our congregation led more than 4,000 to Christ! We didn't need to spend thousands of dollars on advertising because our members caught on to their purpose. "And the lord said unto the servant, Go out into the highways and hedges, and compel them to come in, that my house may be filled."[11]

Television commercials, billboards and newspaper ads will not bring in the amount of people that one "on fire" church member brings! I'm not against effective advertising to provide exposure for God's Strategy House. I've just found that the majority of visitors and new converts come when church members invite them to come.

A church full of soul winners not only increases church membership at an exponential rate, but we become zealous and excited as we fulfill our purpose as believers. We become "doers" of the Word and not just "hearers" as we co-labor together.

Disciple

Converts do not beget converts. Disciples beget converts! The church must have a plan to take new converts through the spiritual maturity process. "Go therefore and make disciples of the nations . . . ."[12] We are commanded to produce disciples! How? That's where the G-MEN strategy will come in.

Send

Once converts are equipped with the message of the Gospel, we must send them out into the harvest. I've read that we "measure the strength of a church by its sending capacity, not its seating capacity."[13] If church members don't preach the message of salvation to the lost, what are we doing? A church's success is measured by its ability to win, disciple and send.

We must understand the purpose for our church. Only then can we accurately measure success, identify areas that need improvement and experience the fulfillment and gratification that comes from knowing we are accomplishing what God intends for us to achieve. Churches grow by a partnership with God and man. "We cannot do it without God and He chose not to do it without us."[14]

Dr. Cole says, "It's a great thing to have faith in God. It is greater that God has faith in us!"

COMMUNICATE THE PURPOSE

In the book entitled, *The Purpose-Driven Church*, in a survey of nearly 1000 churches, a consultant asked, "Why does the church exist?" Most of the members said, "The church's purpose is to take care of my family's and my needs." They had effectively reduced the role of the pastor to keeping the sheep in the "pen" happy. Only 11% said, "The purpose of the church is to win the world for Jesus Christ."[15]

The consultant asked pastors of the same churches why the church exists. The results were the exact opposite. Most pastors, 90%, said the purpose of the church was to win the world. Only 10% said the purpose was caring for members' needs.

What do you believe about the purpose of the church? What do you think your friends or congregation members think?

I asked my staff one day to write in their own words what they deemed the purpose of our church to be. I figured if the leadership doesn't know, the rest of the congregation certainly doesn't know!

We used each staff member's ideas to compose one final purpose statement. "Write the vision, and make it plain upon tables, that he may run that readeth it."[16] Having a purpose statement helps us all communicate our church vision. Our purpose statement is:

"I am doing my part to overcome racial, cultural and denominational barriers to ensure that everyone in my city hears the Gospel; I am fulfilling the Great Commission by mentoring followers to become effective leaders with spiritual integrity."

People must have individual purpose. Couples must have purpose together. Church members must have purpose as a church.

[1] I Peter 5:17
[2] Luke 7:47
[3] Proverbs 29:18
[4] Webster's New World™ College Dictionary, Third Edition, 1997, Simon and Schuster, Inc.
[5] I John 3:8
[6] Genesis 2:15
[7] Genesis 3:1
[8] Romans 5:19
[9] Mark 14:36
[10] Mark 16:15
[11] Luke 14:23
[12] Matthew 28:19 NIV
[13] Warren, *The Purpose-Driven Church*, Zondervan, Grand Rapids, MI, 1995, page 32
[14] Warren, *The Purpose-Driven Church*, Zondervan, Grand Rapids, MI, 1995, page 60
[15] Warren, *The Purpose-Driven Church*, Zondervan, Grand Rapids, MI, 1995, page 15
[16] Habakkuk 2:2

3

Cinching the Net

```
                                    Step Three: Send
                  Step Two: Disciple |
Step One: Win |
```

What's the Problem?

It's one thing to identify your purpose. It's another to fulfill it!

How do we keep the fish inside the boat that we catch in our nets? We can have methods. We need anointing. But will they stay for either?

One method is a two-day intense weekend retreat, which cell church leaders call an "encounter." During our church's first "encounters," thirty men committed to taking the Gospel to the world. Now, because many of those men did what they said they'd do, we have encounters virtually every weekend with new converts who solidify spiritually and get on with the mentoring process. Greg attended one and said, *"The Encounter was one of the most spiritual experiences I have ever been part of. I have never felt the presence of God as strongly as I did there. This was an opportunity to let your guard down, leave your pride and dignity at the door, and experience God as never before! The lessons covered seemed to be the perfect word at the perfect time for everyone there. I will never forget it, and I will recommend it to everyone."*

Greg received an *impartation* of the anointing of Christ's Spirit at that encounter. It's not the weekend meeting, but the *anointing* that breaks the yoke. Many look to the method, and follow the program. But Jesus' *method* never healed anyone. Jesus' *touch* healed them. The method is instant. The touch is constant. The *anointing* abides.

Today signs, wonders and miracles occur all over the world. Gifted preachers and teachers minister on the radio and television almost twenty-four hours a day. People all over the world receive healing and deliverance. But how do we change converts into soul-winning disciples? Only if they stay in church do we have the opportunity. We'll never clean a single fish that jumps back into the sea.

People come in the front door, pray the sinner's prayer and head right out the back door. Drawn by human nature, they go back into the world once they get their answer. Guest evangelists come to our church and we see hundreds of people saved. Drama teams and ministry performance groups come and thousands of people give their lives to Christ, but where are they now? We had 4,000 people saved in one year and yet added only hundreds to the church.

How successful is a fishing trip if a man catches a net full of fish only to find it was full of holes and the fish dropped back into the sea? We must cinch the net!

UPON THIS ROCK

"He saith unto them, But whom say ye that I am? And Simon Peter answered and said, Thou art the Christ, the Son of the living God. And Jesus answered and said unto him, Blessed art thou, Simon Barjona: for flesh and blood hath not revealed it unto thee, but my Father which is in heaven. And I say also unto thee, That thou art Peter, and upon this Rock I will build *my church*; and the gates of hell shall not prevail against it."[1]

Peter had the revelation that Jesus was the Messiah. Jesus called him blessed for it. But once we have the revelation that Jesus is Lord, it's time to build the church. Jesus doesn't intend to save people, then send them on their way. He expects converts to be added to His Church. Each person who recognizes Jesus as the Son of God is to help build the Church.

Revelation of who He is: *The Messiah*
What He came to do: *Destroy the works of the devil*
        Build the church on this revelation.

The Church is not a building. The Church is people. The gates of hell cannot prevail against the people who are planted in the Church, which fulfills Jesus' purpose to destroy the works of the enemy.

"I will build my church," Jesus said.[2] Yet the Bible records that Jesus is now seated at the right hand of the Father.[3] So how will He build His Church? Through His "Body" that is right here on earth. We're called the Body of Christ. Regardless of denominational titles, race, culture or creed, every believer is an intricate part of Christ's Body. As we win souls, impart anointing to them and disciple them by keeping them in our local churches, the Body of Christ grows and Jesus builds His church!

Fruit That Remains

"Ye have not chosen me, but I have chosen you, and ordained you, that ye should go and bring forth fruit, and that your fruit should remain . . . ."[4]

Our fruit, the converts we make, must remain in the church, so we can disciple them. When we disciple converts, we fulfill our purpose. As we fulfill our purpose, Christ's purpose is fulfilled to destroy the works of the enemy.

Our congregation takes the Gospel outside the four walls of our church through "lifestyle evangelism." It's not uncommon for our members to lead someone in the prayer of salvation in the grocery store, at a restaurant or in the mall. As pleasing as it is to see such boldness and winning souls, leading people to Christ only fulfills the first goal.

We are to win, disciple and then send!

People can be saved, but then let's add them to the vision. Let's enable them to do their part. Let's see their lives transformed by the Word of God. "Those that be planted in the house of the Lord shall flourish in the courts of our God."[5] Let's plant converts in the House of God so they can flourish.

How discouraging to host conferences, conduct outreaches, witness and pass out Bible tracts if we never see the result or benefits of our efforts because the people we minister to are gone. We grow weary of working to bring people into the House if we don't see them grow. Events focused on bringing new people to church can become redundant. We must have a purposeful strategy to take converts past step one.

"Surely blessing I will bless thee, and multiplying I will multiply thee."[6] God wants the church multiplying.

As long as converts head out the back door, we might *add* members to the church, but we are not *multiplying* membership as we could. The army of God doesn't increase at the exponential rate we need so we are forced to slow down our visionary efforts due to a lack of manpower.

How Many Souls in a Seed?

In Texas, we are known for our ripe, juicy watermelons. In the middle of a hot summer day, it's a joy to grab a cold melon, break it open, and smell that sweet, cool watermelon aroma.

As I devour the bright red fruit, I pick out the seeds, until all that remains on my plate is a bunch of black seeds floating in sticky watermelon juice. I can count the seeds on my plate. But the truth is, I cannot count the watermelons in a seed!

When a newly-saved Christian is lost to the world, or even to an apathetic, mediocre lifestyle, a seed has been stolen. I can count the seeds stolen, but I cannot count the thousands upon thousands of souls each seed represents. When potential souls are lost, exponential growth is lost for the church. The seeds must be cultivated, discipled, planted in the church.

Would a corporate entity ever pay an employee without a system to evaluate his or her performance? Would they pay a hefty salary and yet not care how that employee is doing their part to generate funds for the company?

We're not employers in the Church, but we still need a way to measure how many lives truly are being transformed and changed through our efforts. If large numbers of converts tend to disappear, have we really done our job? The G-MEN strategy provides the measuring stick we need.

Jesus Recognizes the Need to Have Fruit Remain

"And Jesus went about all the cities and villages, teaching in their synagogues, and preaching the gospel of the kingdom, and healing every sickness and every disease among the people. But when he saw the multitudes, he was moved with compassion on them, because they fainted, and were scattered abroad, as sheep having no shepherd. Then saith he unto his disciples, The harvest truly is plenteous, but the labourers are few; Pray ye therefore the Lord of the harvest, that he will send forth labourers into his harvest."[7]

When people are healed and delivered at church, we shout for joy! We praise God and leave church feeling victorious.

So why is it that after Jesus preached, taught and healed the people, He was sad? He was sad to know that without a shepherd, organizer, servant, laborer, the people would go right back into the very things from which He'd just released them.

The people Jesus ministered to were fainting because they didn't have a pastor, a mentor, a leader. They fainted then and they're still fainting today. Many Christians get saved at the altar, then hop from church to church, conference to conference, until without a shepherd leading them, they faint.

Jesus recognized that good sermons and miracles were not enough. People need to be discipled, and that requires all of us being willing and equipped to implement an effective strategy that will mobilize and train up new converts.

Jesus did not pray for God to bring a harvest of souls. As a matter of fact, He stated that plenty of people are ready to receive the Gospel—"the harvest is plenteous."[8] He prayed for laborers. The real need, He said, is for believers to rise up and minister.

With great purpose, Jesus referred to the lost as a harvest. God told Adam to dress and keep the Garden.[9] God called the very first man to take responsibility for the condition of the world around him. That commandment still stands! Adam was told to tend a garden. Jesus prayed for us to tend the harvest. The Body of Christ is to walk in God-given authority against the devil.

Our thoughts must focus on taking over the world with the Gospel. The "missing link" in humanity today is not an ape-man creature. It is a man with the nature of God inside him that enables him to lead like Jesus leads, with boldness and love. Jesus had a mindset to "take over." So do we. "For the earnest expectation of the creature waiteth for the manifestation of the sons of God."[10]

We cinch the net by checking first for holes, hoisting our catch into the boat, and keeping the fish from sliding back into the waters. We win souls, then focus on discipling them in order to send them. That's the final strategy!

[1] Matthew 16:15-18 (Italics mine)
[2] Matthew 16:18
[3] Hebrews 10:12
[4] John 15:16
[5] Psalms 92:13
[6] Hebrews 6:14
[7] Matthew 9:35-38
[8] Matthew 9:37
[9] Genesis 2:15
[10] Romans 8:19

4

PLAN: SAVE THE HEAD

Ben Kinchlow wrote that "Being a male is a matter of birth. Being a man is a matter of choice." Men are making that choice every day under the G-MEN strategy. A brother wrote recently:

> *Being mentored has changed me. I have learned to take responsibility for what happens with my family and in my home. I can no longer hang my wife out to dry, so to speak. I cannot blame her for everything that goes wrong. I need to be the foundation in my home for my wife and my kids. My wife is much happier when she doesn't get blamed when something goes wrong!*
>
> *I have also learned to be man enough to listen and let my mentor tell me when I mess up. Recently, I let an old addiction come back into my house and it hurt my wife deeply. My mentor flat out told me how I messed up and what to do to get my house back in order. With my wife, we are getting victory in this. We are not there yet, but we are on our way.*

It's been said, "Lead your life so you're not ashamed to sell the family parrot to the town gossip." Many of us, particularly men, are nowhere near this measure. We have to make a purposeful choice to be men, to act like men in public as well as in private.

CHRIST, OUR EXAMPLE

Manhood and Christlikeness are synonymous, Dr. Cole says. The more men understand *who they are in Christ,* the more of a *man* they become. God constantly uses the relationship of Christ to the church to show men and women their responsibilities and roles toward one another.

"For the husband is the head of the wife, even as Christ is the head of the church: and he is the Saviour of the body. Therefore as the church is subject unto Christ, so let the wives be to their own husbands in every thing. Husbands, love your wives, even as Christ also loved the church, and gave himself for it."[1]

A man cannot understand what it means to be the *head* of his wife until he understands how Christ is the *head* of the Church. And the more a man understands how Christ loves and cares for the Church, the more he is able to comprehend what it means to love his wife as Christ loves the Church.

Men's ability to function as the priests of their homes is directly related to their understanding of Christ. Family unity will not exist until the man is restored and the man cannot be maximized until Jesus is *Lord* of his life. Many Christians know Jesus as their Savior, but making Jesus our Lord means we die to our personal agendas and serve Him with full submission and compliance.

The Bible instructs husbands to live and dwell with their wives according to knowledge.[2] Since all knowledge and wisdom comes from God, I realized that if I couldn't get along with my wife it was because I didn't have the knowledge I needed. I could no longer blame her when God explicitly told me to get knowledge from Him to live with her.

God's plan for the harvest starts with the restoration of men as laborers and leaders. As men learn to embrace their role as godly husbands and fathers, and they accept responsibility for the spiritual condition of the world around them, we truly can eliminate the missing link that has destabilized the Body of Christ for so long!

Why did I create a G-MEN strategy rather than G-women? Dr. David Yonggi Cho, pastor of the largest church on earth has 47,000 women leading cell groups! It must be working! Yet I discovered that women and children suffer when I minister to them and get them healed and delivered, but send them home to an unregenerate man. By majoring in men, the men minister to their wives and children, and the whole family benefits. I've found that men must be encouraged, taught, mentored, and led to take their place of Godly leadership in the home and church. The man is literally the missing link.

WHAT ABOUT WOMEN?

Since the beginning of time, the devil has taken truths and twisted them to deceive people. Just as God is the same yesterday, today and forever, the devil hasn't changed a bit either. He loves to put people in bondage—the men, the women, the children—he's not picky!

Looking at this image, some people see a beautiful young woman. Others see an elderly depressed woman. The truth is, we perceive life through our own experiences. We often see things as *we* are, not as *they* are.

Truth and reality are synonymous. Perceptions alone don't cut it. To walk in reality, we must be diligent in pursuing truth.

The Bible refers to women as the "weaker vessel," but this doesn't mean she is inferior or inadequate to a man.[3] It means she is precious and to be valued. Pastor Walter Hallam says men are like plastic everyday dishes and women are like fine china. We may toss our plastic containers into the dishwasher and store them in stacks under a kitchen cabinet, but that's not how we handle china. We hand wash china with great care and marvel at its beauty.

The Bible says men must give honor to their wives. If they don't, their prayers will be hindered.[4] Sounds harsh, but that's how serious God is about the way women are treated! In other words, God is saying, "Son, until you learn to treat my precious daughter right, I refuse to bless you."

GUIDE, GUARD AND GOVERN

Dr. Cole teaches in his curriculum, *Majoring In Men*, that men are to guide, guard and govern their families. This provides a spiritual covering for his wife and children.

1. Guide

A man guides his family by his Christlike example. He reacts with the nature of Christ when faced with the daily challenges of life. A husband seeks God and shares revelations with his wife that builds confidence in her because she knows he is hearing from God. His spiritual guidance gives her peace of mind. She rests assured that he is taking responsibility for his part in running the household.

2. Guard

A husband protects his wife spiritually by praying for her and with her. He protects her physically by providing shelter, food, clothing and taking responsibility for her wellbeing. A husband protects his wife emotionally by encouraging her, exhorting her, appreciating her and listening to what matters to her and what she needs. He is committed to seeing his wife achieve her destiny in Christ. He is an extension of the love of the Father in her life and the children come to understand God's love through him.

3. *Govern*

A man takes responsibility for the spiritual and physical condition of his home. He makes decisions based on the Word and gives his family direction based on Biblical patterns and principles. The husband is willing to be the problem-solver for his family, not passing blame and stress to his wife. He ensures that God's commands are carried out in the home.

A man is the *covering* of his home. Just as the roof of a house prevents storms from disturbing the climate inside, a Godly man protects his family and doesn't allow the enemies' devices and schemes to get past him to his wife and children. He is equipped and anointed to handle the storms of life. He ensures his family remains in peace and safety.

On the other hand, a roof can endure rain, wind and hail, as long as the rafters don't collapse. But even something as durable as a rooftop must be supported. A husband's ability to cover his home collapses when his wife refuses to support him. He can take attacks outside of the home and he can stand against spiritual battles the devil sends, but when his own wife strikes at him with constant complaints, correction and condemnation, the roof can cave in.

A husband needs his wife's support. Even when he makes mistakes and is in need of revelation, having rafters in place provides strength for him. The *two* become *one*. They are not each other's problem. The devil is their problem together, and unity is the answer.

The foundation of the house keeps the entire structure sturdy. The Word of God is the ultimate underpinning for our marriages. All disagreements can be settled by simply asking, "What does the Bible say about this situation?" If God's Word is given the highest priority in the home, the house will never collapse!

A woman named Angela describes the change in her house this way:

> My husband and I used to come home from work and watch television for hours. Since he started attending mentoring, we've turned off the TV and started reading the Word and praying together! I have watched as the characteristics of a leader have gradually developed in my husband and I am thrilled to have a "maximized man" loving me and supporting me.

Taken to extremes, male *spectators* and male *dictators* emerge, neither of which describe a *maximized* man. A Christlike man leads by following what Christ said, "let he who is greatest among you be servant of all."[5] We lead by serving, by looking out for the interests of others, by meeting the needs of others.

The man can make decisions he feels are in the best interest of God's will for the household, but he will give an account to God for the outcome of those decisions. A man who understands this does not take his role as the head of the household lightly. A woman who understands the accountability God expects from her husband will do everything she can to support him. Not threatened by her husband's role of leadership, she is instead grateful.

Wendy is one of our members who was discipled with her husband. She wrote:

> When I first heard about the men's mentoring program, I must admit, I was skeptical. Since my husband and I were both baby Christians, I thought his involvement with mentoring would only make it obvious how dysfunctional our marriage was. I did not want him to hear about how

a woman of God should treat a man, only to see that I fell short of those expectations.

Well, my concerns were all wrong! The more my husband learned, the more Christlike he became, which helped me to be the woman of God I needed to be. Working on the curriculum together every week gave us a steady dose of marital improvement and in time, our lives were dramatically changed. I thank God for the G-MEN strategy every day because I now have a maximized husband and a rejuvenated marriage!

The mentoring program focuses on men, but it directs their attention to loving their wives. Women who love Christ love having a Christlike husband. Women are the first and most direct beneficiaries of the G-MEN strategy. One of our leaders' wives became a true believer. Joni writes:

God has done a divine reversal by taking our dry and lifeless marriage and turning it into a life-giving union. God has taken what we had given up on and made it something worth working on! Not only has our marriage been resurrected, but our family unit has been reunited. God is now able to work in our lives by my decision to allow my husband to guide, guard and govern our home. Through our obedience to the Word of God, my husband has stepped into position directly beneath Christ.

THE NEED FOR MEN TO LEAD

From the time of Adam's fall, through the ordination of Abraham, Moses, Joseph, Sampson, David and Jesus, God has used men as laborers and leaders. Women can be spiritual giants, as was Deborah the judge and Joanna who supported Jesus. Both men and women are called to acquire the attributes of godliness. But, for too long men have pushed women into the position of head of the household in order to avoid the accountability of making decisions.

One of the main attributes of a man of God is that he is decisive! God's redemptive plan is to have men exercise decision-making as kings and priests in the Kingdom of God. All women want their mate to make decisions, take initiative and accept an active role running the many facets of a household.

When men decline to function in their God-given role of leadership, women are sucked into the vacuum. Man's refusal to walk in the authority God gave him, and woman's tendency to compensate for his lack of leadership, plays out in the home, the church and society.

When men step out in faith for their families, miracles happen. Three years ago, the daughter of a man named Kyle was diagnosed with a liver condition. It caused such severe itching and pain, she would literally pull her hair out. The doctors could do nothing except prescribe a liver transplant.

Many men in similar situations sit in helpless frustration, not knowing what to do. They lash out at their wives, or expect the wife to call her prayer group. But Kyle acted like a man. He and his wife stood on the Word of God and believed for a miracle. Kyle brought his daughter to the altar at church for prayer. Within weeks, she had no itching or symptoms. Soon she was sleeping through the night, pain-free and completely healed.

Kyle took leadership, decided to stand on the Word with his wife, and both wife and daughter were the beneficiaries of his faith.

THE AXEHEAD

The typical state of men and women in the home today is pathetic. Sitcoms, films and song lyrics reflect as well as perpetuate our sorry condition. Many church members are no different from the rest of society. The twenty-first century Church is often typified by women dragging their husbands and children to church and husbands grudging a few dollars in the offering plate to pay penance. The problem is that there is no head!

"And the sons of the prophets said unto Elisha, Behold now, the place where we dwell with thee is too straight for us. Let us go, we pray thee, unto Jordan, and take thence every man a beam, and let us make us a place there, where we may dwell. And he answered, Go ye. And one said, Be content, I pray thee, and go with thy servants. And he answered, I will go. So he went with them. And when they came to Jordan, they cut down wood. But as one was felling a beam, the axe head fell into the water: and he cried, and said, Alas, master! for it was borrowed. And the man of God said, Where fell it? And he shewed him the place. And he cut down a stick, and cast it in thither; and the iron did swim. Therefore said he, Take it up to thee. And he put out his hand, and took it."[6]

In this passage, men building a church recognized that they needed a bigger building. They had outgrown their current facility and wanted to expand, so they went to the Jordan to cut trees. In Biblical types and shadows, the Jordan always represents a place of decision. These men made a *decision* to build the church.

As the men cut down beams for their new House of God, one man's axe head fell into the water and sank, leaving him with just an axe handle. Like an axe handle with no head, so is a family where the head of the household has fallen away from his responsibility as the priest of his home, only to sink beneath apathy and self-justification. He lies dormant at the bottom of his Jordan, avoiding his role as the decision maker.

How much longer would it take to cut a tree and build a church using only an axe *handle*? For the same reason, the

Body of Christ has not made the progress it needs to because true men have not risen up to participate and support the work of the Lord.

The church is weak today because we've built it with half a tool—axe *handles!* The axe *handle* gives the axe *head* the leverage and strength of movement to fell the tree. But the axe *handle* was never meant to deliver the striking blow! The axe *head* was designed to cut wood! *Axe handle* represents the female and *axe head* represents the male.

The sunken axe head that prevented the man from continuing his work was the *missing link* in building the church. Elisha said, "throw a stick in the water!" and a miracle happened. The axe head swam to the surface. In the same way, when men rise to the surface, the missing link is eliminated.

But how do we get men to "swim back up to the top"? The stick in the water is a type of the Cross. All creation fell when Adam fell. However, all creation was saved when Jesus went to the "stick" and Calvary's Cross was thrown into the sea of humanity. Jesus made a way for man to ascend to Heaven through Him.

Like the axe head that miraculously swam to the water's surface, when men gain a revelation of who Jesus is, they rise up to the challenge of Godly leadership. This equips the Body to build the Church in the manner in which God intended—in power! It takes maximized, godly men to stand in the place of decision and save other men, women and families that are drowning.

Look at the blessing to the home when men take the position at the *head:*

> *My husband was in mentoring before we married. He learned how to be the priest of the home before we ever said "I do." When my husband comes home from mentoring, he tells me what God spoke to him during the meeting. He*

always gets such powerful revelations about being a loving husband that I find myself seeking God to show me how to be a better wife! He inspires me to become more of a woman of God and it blesses me to see that he is willing to make such a huge investment in our marriage. – Laura

MARRIAGE, AN ILLUSTRATED SERMON

God uses the marriage relationship to teach us about His nature and character. As we struggle to understand the opposite sex, we begin to understand the nature of God—Whose name, "El Shaddai," means *"the many breasted one."* Both male and female are made in God's image, so both reflect the nature of God. In marriage, we learn more about Him by learning more about our spouses.

Just the difference in physical makeup between males and females makes it apparent that men are anatomically made to be *givers,* while women are anatomically created to be *receivers* and *nurturers.* The male gives the seed and the woman receives it, nurtures it for nine months and then gives birth. As we work together to understand each other, women learn how to *give* assertively, and men learn how to *receive* and *nurture.*

As the Body of Christ, we must learn how to *give* to God and how to *receive* from God. By balancing those two areas, our relationship with God flourishes! My wife and I studied our Biblical roles and came to understand our purpose as a ministry team. This gave me a great sense of patience and direction for my wife and family.

When husbands and wives both reflect God's glory in their roles and responsibilities, the entire family comes under the headship of Jesus Christ. This unity brings us under God's *commanded* blessing.

"Behold, how good and how pleasant it is for brethren to dwell together in unity! It is like the precious ointment upon the head, that ran down upon the beard, even Aaron's beard: that went down to the skirts of his garments; As the dew of Hermon, and as the dew that descended upon the mountains of Zion: for there the Lord commanded the blessing, even life forevermore."[7]

God's anointing and blessing flows through the head to the entire household. When this divine order is carried out, peace reigns in the home. With unity restored, God commands His blessing. An attempt to achieve unity without an established order becomes nothing more than fellowship, and leaves a church ill-equipped to destroy the works of the enemy.

When order is established, the anointing flows down a supernatural channel and results in miracles, signs and wonders.

Christlike men are the *missing link* the devil has attacked to keep families unfulfilled and unstable. A church is only as strong as its members, so its members must come to understand God's plan for the family. The roof and walls of a building will collapse if the foundation is not sturdy enough to support them. Church members will collapse under the weight of the ministry if they don't have a sturdy foundation of truth.

"If the foundation be destroyed, what can the righteous do?"[8] On that foundational Rock (Jesus), unity of purpose is being established and the commanded blessing is coming to pass.

It's not coincidence when we see miraculous increase in our services and cities. It's the fulfillment of scripture. A foundation has been laid, sturdy enough for the work of the ministry.

[1] Ephesians 5:23
[2] I Peter 3:7
[3] I Peter 3:7
[4] I Peter 3:7
[5] Matthew 23:11
[6] II Kings 6:1-7
[7] Psalm 133:3
[8] Psalm 11:3

5

Spiritual Unemployment

But watch thou in all things, endure afflictions, do the work of an evangelist, make full proof of thy ministry.[1]

Yes, soul-winning is our thrust, but we recognize also that God didn't tell everyone to *be* an evangelist. He said to do the *work* of an evangelist. What is the work of an evangelist? It's to tell people about Jesus, lead them to Christ and help build the church. As believers, we have been commanded to take the Gospel to our neighborhood, city, nation and the world.

Who is going to do it? I tell the men to do it! Does this mean women aren't called to win souls and minister to the lost? Of course not! God does not esteem one gender over another.[2]

Women are well equipped for lifestyle evangelism because women are typically great at relationships. It's not an abundance of females in the Body of Christ that's a problem today. It's the lack of male participation that has slowed us down! From reports I've read over the years, the average church congregation is still 80% female and 20% male. The harvest is plenteous, but the *men* are few! "Adam, where art thou?"

Men Must Produce

A man's creativity, productivity and ability gives him worth, value, and a sense of dignity. For that reason, unemployment is a devastating, soul-damaging condition, and one of the greatest stresses in a man's life. A man who can't exercise his ability to be productive and earn money for his family, tends to lose his sense of worth.

46

Have you ever wondered why crime is so high in low-income areas? It's not because people who live there have less morals or ethics. It's because unemployment tends to be as high as 25% to 30% in such areas, which is what makes them low income.

A man without a job or a means of maximizing his creativity or abilities will search for another outlet to express himself, often illegally. The reason why a young man deals drugs on the street is because he finds fulfillment and value in his ability to earn money. He also gets to use his creativity to avoid the law and that adds to his feeling of satisfaction.

We can't just tell a man to quit dealing drugs and not give him a job. Somehow, somewhere, he desires an outlet for his ability, creativity and productivity. When a man walks down the street with a hundred-dollar bill in his pocket, he feels he has it made. But a man without a penny to his name feels emasculated. Men who are unemployed, whose wives become dependent on the welfare system, don't even have the satisfaction of relationship. Her source of provision becomes the government instead of her husband.

THE GOSPEL WELFARE SYSTEM

Now look at the rate of *spiritual* unemployment in the church. We shudder when society's unemployment rises into two digits. But in the church, we settle for unemployment as high as 80% to 95%!

Spiritually unemployed people in the church experience the same loss of value as unemployed people in the world. When 80% of the people are not doing the work of an evangelist, the majority of the congregation depends on the pastor, like a gospel welfare system.

In a gospel welfare system, the pastor becomes the source for all revelation and spiritual help. I'm a minister, but I won't deny that some ministers perpetuate dependency because they get a feeling of importance. But ministers of the *whole* gospel teach the five-fold ministries out of Ephesians that equip the Body for the work of the ministry.

The Church depends on *every* member doing the work of an evangelist. Church members *must* take responsibility for the move of God in the local church. I learned this principle first from Dr. Cole's book *Strong Men in Tough Times,* but I've witnessed it, experienced it, and preached it so much, it's mine now! It's just so true.

Spiritually unemployed people are the most likely to become dissatisfied with the church and turn to illicit, ungodly, even illegal sources of pleasure. The Church overall is struggling with a plague of immorality, due in large measure to the high spiritual unemployment rate. Church members with little to do spend their time flirting with sin until they fall right into it.

A church full of spiritually employed members accomplishes the vision at a much faster pace, with a fraction of the need for counseling and crisis management. By mobilizing *men* to do their share of the work, we work *smarter,* not *harder.* We need members to move from the pew to the plow. It starts by employing the men.

This, again, is not to minimize the service of women. No way! Women are shouldering much of the load today because of the absence of men. We need the head, the laborer, doing his part. Men are to be *setting* the example for their family, and instead they are just *sitting.* Men, let's get off the bench and get in the game!

A great understanding of this is that men (Adam) were the first laborers put into the garden to till it or work the harvest! God in His infinite wisdom took Eve out of Adam and made a statement—"The two shall become one." We are truly the "laborer" when we are unified and one together in the harvest. The most efficient laborer in the harvest is the husband and wife as one working together. However, until the man gets involved—axe handle!

THE COMPUTER MAN

Never was this made more real to me than with a man named Greg. Greg came to church because his wife begged him. He was a career man, highly skilled in computers and very analytical. After attending a church service at PowerHouse, he could not comprehend why people were so happy. He insisted it was fake, that church members could not possibly be so zealous and joyful. He convinced himself it was all an act to get him to join the church.

One day, one of the men I mentor asked Greg to help with the church's computers. Greg agreed. By working with us, he began to see that we were real. Our joy was genuine. His concerns about the church dissipated and over time, by using his talents and skills in the House, Greg changed spiritually. Putting his hand to the plow gave him a sense of value, worth and belonging to the vision. He developed a mindset of ownership for the ministry because his gifts benefited the House! By becoming spiritually employed, Greg became spiritually alive. He is now one of the most productive home group leaders in our church and he is mentoring several men—all analytical types like him!

THE FIVE-FOLD MINISTRY

As five-fold ministers, our focus must be to mature, or perfect, other saints. We are to do more than train people to come to church, sit on the bench and tithe. We are to equip others for the work of the ministry. We disciple converts, then send them to evangelize within their sphere of influence.

"And he gave some, apostles; and some, prophets; and some, evangelists; and some, pastors and teachers; For the perfecting of the saints, for the work of the ministry, for the edifying of the body of Christ."[3]

I may have established a ministry, but it is not my ministry. The ministry belongs to every member of the church. God never intended for any one person to do the work of the ministry. Running a local church consists of obtaining and maintaining members, which is the job of the saints. One person, or even a large, efficient staff, cannot do all the work, nor should anyone want to! As men and women serve, they find purpose within the church vision. As they find work that fulfills purpose, they become spiritually employed. As they're employed, they are more fulfilled, and so forth.

The next line of that passage reads, "Till we all come in the unity of the faith, and of the knowledge of the Son of God, unto a perfect man, unto the measure of the stature of the fullness of Christ."[4]

The Word does not say, "until we come into the unity of the doctrine." We grow in *faith*. Faith comes by hearing the Word of God, so we must mature in the Word. We, as five-fold ministers, must teach about the Son of God so others will have knowledge of Jesus, and be transformed into a perfect man, which is Christlike.

This starts by teaching men. When we restore order in the family, and the family lines up under the headship of Jesus Christ, we can restore the same measure of the anointing in which Jesus walked. Isolated miracles occur here and there, but Jesus had miracles every time. His ability to impart the anointing was consistent. The Body of Christ needs that same consistency of God's power in our walk with the Lord today.

The Apostle Paul goes on to say, "That we henceforth be no more children, tossed to and fro, and carried about with every wind of doctrine, by the sleight of men, and cunning craftiness, whereby they lie in wait to deceive."[5]

We must disciple new converts so the devil cannot deceive them. We must raise up spiritual adults who have passed the ignorance of childhood. Our job as five-fold ministers is to exhibit and model the nature of Christ, and love as spiritual mothers and fathers, so converts can grow up and do something for the Kingdom of God, rather than just for themselves.

"But speaking the truth in love," Paul continues, "may grow up into him in all things, which is the head, even Christ."[6]

How do we spiritually mature people? We speak the truth in love. How do we speak the truth in love? Through relationship. One of the biggest deceptive devices in the Church is offense. Offense occurs when people don't have enough relationship to know the person speaking truth to them, so they take it wrong. We need to speak the truth, but it can kill people if they do not have relationship with us or know that we love them. *People do not care how much you know until they know how much you care.*

True mentoring demonstrates unconditional love. That *kind of* relationship takes time to build. As we meet weekly and take the time to call and check up on people, that bond is formed. We all need someone we can submit to and receive the truth from, in love. Truth is essential to spiritual growth. When we quit receiving truth, we quit growing.

Paul ends this particular passage with, "From whom the whole body fitly joined together and compacted by that which every joint supplieth, according to the effectual working in the measure of every part, maketh increase of the body unto the edifying of itself in love."[7]

God desires increase. He loves people and hates the devil, and the devil is after God's people. The increase of God's people is His heart and purpose. To bring people out of darkness and into His marvelous light destroys the works of the enemy and builds the Church. Edifying and building the Body of Christ is what God does best.

We must seize every opportunity to grow the Church. We must communicate the Gospel to twenty-first century beings. While the methods may change to accommodate society, the message never changes. Dr. Cole says, "Change is the only constant in maturity." Let's be pliable enough to understand how God is going to catch fish today and what He will use for a net in this hour.

Everything God touches multiplies. God's plan is very plain. He's given the five-fold ministry so we can mature the Body of Christ. Then all saints can become spiritually employed and *do the work of the ministry,* which edifies the Body, until we come into the perfect man, which is Jesus Christ. Then we can begin to do what Jesus did with the same power, anointing and relationship He had with the Father.

MAKING THE MOST OF THE FIVE-FOLD MINISTRY

For years, I've seen pastors hesitate to bring prophets, evangelists, apostles and teachers into their churches because they cannot identify long-term benefits of those ministries. So, an evangelist who operates in the gift of the working of miracles comes to church and the power of God falls on everyone. Then what? A prophet of God comes and gives out prophecies to the entire congregation. What's next? A well-known teacher comes to minister and his "fan club" travels to your church to see him and they never come back again. What good is that?

We must focus on *purpose*. God created every ministry gift to work together in unity of purpose. What does a pastor have in common with a prophet? They are both called to build the church. Five-fold ministers bring new families into the church and deposit a unique anointing, but it's up to the local church to have a plan or structure in place to make the most of that event.

The G-MEN strategy capitalizes on the five-fold gifts and establishes a God-centered relationship between the church and the five-fold ministries. The strategy also helps pastors develop vision and purpose to orchestrate what the church needs from the five-fold ministry.

The tape and notes of the five-fold minister that just visited your church will now be assimilated throughout your leadership and body through the weekly mentorship meetings in which the tape and notes are rubbed into the protégé. This is how the five-fold gifts' seed is retained in the church and value is established.

[1] II Timothy 4:5
[2] Genesis 2:24
[3] Ephesians 4:11-12
[4] Ephesians 4:13
[5] Ephesians 4:14
[6] Ephesians 4:15
[7] Ephesians 4:16

6

STRATEGY: G-MEN

President Roosevelt gave a directive to build the Panama Canal in an effort to improve the rate of commerce. Thousands were employed for the job. While progress was being made, it was not at the rate he had intended, so he looked into the matter and was appalled at what he discovered.

The project lacked efficiency because the living conditions of the men were so deplorable that deadly malaria was sweeping through the camp and killing the workers. He realized that more men were dying trying to build the canal than soldiers were dying in the war.

Roosevelt redirected his efforts to improve the environment and surroundings for the men in Panama. They stopped working on the canal and cleaned the streets, rerouted sewers, cut the grass and installed hanging mosquito nets in the sleeping quarters. These reformations abolished malaria and work on the canal began again without the hindrance of sickness and death. The men were then able to focus on the goal set before them and they completed the Panama Canal in record time.

This is similar to what has manifested in the Church. We were given a mandate from God, a Great Commission, to "Go into all the world and preach the Gospel."[1] We were commanded to build a canal that would allow God's love and the message of salvation to flow to unsaved humanity. While we have been busy "having church" there has been a plague in the land that we have failed to realize. The spiritual condition of men is unacceptable. The reason for their condition is because they do not have a spiritual father to mentor and disciple them. The attributes of Christ are not being formed in men, so consequently, the laborer, the man, has not done his part to further the move of God in this hour.

I believe God has been so tired of losing men to mediocrity that He dropped a revelation into a few men's hearts and declared that it is time to defeat the disease. What we must do is stop, re-evaluate the condition of men and deal with the problem of the missing link so we can open the floodgates to the power of a spiritual canal and accomplish God's plan to win back His man!

As we focus our efforts on restoring men and lining up the family in God's intended order for victory, we create a canal of spiritual maturity that allows the anointing to flow more effectively and efficiently. "Let all things be done decently and in order."[2] This restoration of order will open up the floodgates of God's blessings so we can take the world for Jesus.

Churches often choose to meet members' needs by implementing programs for special interest groups. There's women's ministry, youth ministry, children's ministry, marital counseling programs, and so forth. All of these ministries are beneficial, but have we first gone straight to the head? Since men are given the commandment to be the shepherd of their home and they are held accountable to oversee and care for their wife and children, doesn't it make sense to *focus* our *efforts* on maturing and developing Christlike men?

Perhaps as much as 60% of church programs wouldn't be needed if men were taking care of their homes. We could do the "God things," not just "good things."

All groups can be "fixed" by focusing on one group. Godly men can minister to the needs of others once they understand their mandate from God. A Christlike man who guides, guards and governs his household with Godly wisdom will minister to the needs of his family far more effectively than any church program.

Men Need a Father

An astounding **61%** of the households in America today are fatherless! How damaging it is to have a nation full of "absentee fathers!"

- **63%** of youth suicides are from fatherless homes.
  (Source: U.S. D.H.H.S. Bureau of the Census)

- **90%** of all homeless and runaway children are from fatherless homes.
  (Source: U.S. D.H.H.S. Bureau of the Census)

- **85%** of all children that exhibit behavioral disorders come from fatherless homes.
  (Source: Center for Disease Control)

- **80%** of rapists motivated with displaced anger come from fatherless homes.
  (Source: Criminal Justice & Behavior, Vol. 14, p. 403-26, 1978)

- **71%** of all high school dropouts come from fatherless homes.
  (Source: National Principals Association Report on the State of High Schools)

- **75%** of all adolescent patients in chemical abuse centers come from fatherless homes.
  (Rainbows For All God's Children)

˅ 70% of juveniles in state-operated institutions come from fatherless homes.

(Source: U.S. Dept. of Justice, Special Report, Sept. 1998)

˅ 85% of all youths sitting in prisons grew up in a fatherless home.

(Source: Fulton Co. Georgia jail populations, Texas Dept. of Corrections, 1992)

In the homes that do have fathers, one statistic I read said the average American father gives only thirty-five seconds of his undivided attention to his children each day. Yet in the Bible we read that in the last days God will "turn the hearts of the fathers to the children and the hearts of the children to the fathers."[3] How can this be in such a fatherless nation? In this hour, God is calling men to rise up as spiritual fathers and instruct other men in the Word through relationship and accountability.

If the guidance and support of a father plays such an important role in our ability to function in the world, how much more do we need a man of God to train us up in spiritual things? Ideally, our natural fathers would have modeled Christ for us and been the one to raise us up in the ways of the Lord, but most of us did not have that example growing up.

Even if we did have a father in the home, we most likely did not see him love our mother as Christ loves the Church, and we probably did not see an example of a laborer in the move of God. Our idea of manhood was likely distorted by our father's example and our mind was conditioned to base our masculinity on the world's standards, which directly oppose God's definition of a man. "There is a way that seemeth right unto a man, but the end thereof are the ways of death."[4] As men, we must replace ungodly thought patterns about our role as men, with the truth of God's Word.

"For when for the time ye ought to be teachers, ye have need that one teach you again which be the first principles of the oracles of God; and are become such as have need of milk, and not of strong meat. For every one that useth milk is unskillful in the word of righteousness: for he is a babe. But strong meat belongeth to them that are of full age, even those who by reason of use have their senses exercised to discern both good and evil."[5]

We shouldn't have to re-teach the basics because fathers should have taught us the Word while we were growing up and held us accountable so that our generation could have built upon the advances they made. Instead, God's original plan for the man, the priest of his home, to train his sons to be Christlike has not been carried out in the home . . . until now.

God is calling pastors to do more for men than preach from the pulpit. We are to birth spiritual sons. "I write not these things to shame you, but as my beloved sons I warn you. For though ye have ten thousand instructors in Christ, *yet have ye not many fathers*: for in Christ Jesus I have begotten you through the gospel."[6]

A teacher prepares a lesson, teaches the material and then leaves it up to the student to make use of that teaching. A father, however, wants to know you understand what has been taught because he has a *personal* interest and desire to see you succeed. Fathers model success. They do not just teach about love, they live it. More is *caught* than *taught*. They know their sons and care about them and children are motivated by the confidence their father has in them. It is not enough to teach the Word to men. We have to father them through the Gospel as Paul did.

My Fathers

I've had three men make deep deposits in my life. My spiritual father is Edwin Louis Cole. He has availed himself to me and I'm not even sure why. He has definitely influenced my life with his books, tapes and ministry. He encourages me with letters and phone calls just at the right moment. I have an assurance that if I ever have a hard time hearing from God on an issue, I can call Dr. Cole for ministry.

I made up my mind when Dr. Cole first started speaking into my life that I was going to adhere to whatever he said—whether I liked it or not. That has been the key to why this mentoring relationship has been beneficial. I have given Dr. Cole the right to cut me and I never allow myself to get offended. After all, I prayed for direction and wisdom and God chose Dr. Cole as a vehicle in my life to deliver the truth. Why would I not heed his advice?

Dr. Cole is my spiritual father, but he is not my best friend. I have kept him in a position of honor so I will always be able to receive from him. I've made a point never to cross the line of the Texas "good ole' boy" or become too familiar. We all need fathers and we all need friends—we don't need to mix the two.

My natural father, Gayle Watkins, was a real influence in my life as well. He taught me discipline and toughness and I love him for that. My dad was an All-American athlete at Baylor University in Waco, Texas. As a young boy, I used to love when we would sit on the porch and he would tell me stories.

My Dad's heroic accounts shaped my dreams and I started to see myself as an All-American. I grew up believing there was something magical about being related to a champion like him. I felt there was something in the blood that qualified me to be a winner. "As a man thinks in his heart, so is he."[7]

I thank God for the mindset of victory that my Dad instilled in me. Today, I still believe I am an overcomer and winner because of the blood, only now I know it's not Watkins' blood that makes me victorious—it's the blood of the Lamb. I now find myself telling my sons stories like my dad used to tell me, and you know what? They sit still, pay attention and love that bonding time together. Thanks, Dad.

I also consider Pastor Walter Hallam, Founder and Senior Pastor of Abundant Life Christian Center in LaMarque, Texas, to have been a great influence in my spiritual upbringing. He hired me from the secular world of coaching and taught me valuable concepts in ministry. He has made himself available to me since I started pastoring and I am very grateful for that.

"Where no counsel is, the people fall: but in the multitude of counselors there is safety."[8]

God has blessed me with men of God who have loved me throughout my walk of faith. It has made all the difference in the world and that is why I am so passionate about the concept of submitting to a spiritual father. I've experienced the security that comes from having a mentor and I have seen firsthand how God uses those relationships to mold and mature us.

JESUS PROVIDES A MODEL

Jesus recognized the great need for people to have shepherds. They needed spiritual fathers to care for them after they were preached to, taught and healed. Jesus also gave us the strategy to make that possible.

"And when he had called unto him his twelve disciples, he gave them power against unclean spirits, to cast them out, and to heal all manner of sickness and all manner of disease."[9]

Jesus' method to minister to the multitudes was to disciple twelve men and send them into the harvest. He preached to multitudes, but He mentored only twelve. He spent all three years of His ministry as a spiritual father to those men. The more they became like Him, the more Jesus was able to *duplicate* His efforts. "Imitation is the greatest form of flattery." Scripture says Jesus gave us power to imitate Him. We exercise that power by duplicating the Word, by duplicating ourselves.

My G-Men

I have twelve men that meet with me once a week. All I do is try to teach them everything I know. As they combine the revelations they already know with the additional Biblical insight I give them, they become equipped to do everything I have done and greater.

Jesus said, "Verily, verily, I say unto you, He that believeth on me, the works that I do shall he do also; and greater works than these shall he do; because I go unto my Father."[10]

I have a covenant and pact with my men that says we're in this for life. They can call me anytime and I can call them because we have a relationship deeper than that of an instructor to a student. These men appreciate the time I take to train them up spiritually. The value they place on God's Word drives them to submit to this system of discipleship and support the ministry with their whole hearts.

But I not only teach them, I model and live the victorious life of Christ in front of them. They learn by watching how I handle situations. Dr. Cole says, "A father's responsibility is not to make his children's decisions, but to let the child watch him make his."

Multiplication

Remember what we read in Hebrews, "Surely blessing I will bless thee, and multiplying I will multiply thee."[11]

In the beginning, my wife, Rose, my son, Cole, and I knocked on doors, communicating the vision God had given me to start my church. My son Grant came later. The work was hot and tiring. We were only able to reach about 50 homes in a couple of hours. I remember thinking, "How many more homes could I hit if I had 10 more people helping?" It's common sense that "many hands make little work."

The mentoring program multiplies ministry efforts.

The men I mentor have twelve men in the church they mentor and disciple. Those men each mentor twelve more men. In just three generations of salvations, or levels of mentoring, there is potential for 1,728 men to plug into the church vision and submit to a spiritual father! With that many men, and their wives and children alongside them, you can imagine how fast we are now able to carry out the vision.

Far from shepherding, discipleship, network marketing, cults or any other schemes that have descended into manipulation or trickery over the years, our simple mentoring program is a mutually-beneficial, shared resource whereby we seek out the Lord's direction and leadership together. It's like any kind of coaching, where a group submits to the leadership of a coach who evaluates their play. Team sports and classroom training are well-accepted means of imparting wisdom to others. That's all mentoring is.

Truth is always more *caught* than *taught*. Through mentorship, the anointing is imparted to men. They are rubbed with the Word until it sinks in deeply, and changes the lives and families of those men.

Through mentoring, men come to understand my heart and vision as well. God has allowed me to greatly multiply my efforts. Not only that, their wives are thrilled with the transformation taking place at home. The men minister to their families the way God intends for them to, so their families receive the first fruits, the best benefits, of the mentoring process.

The men become accountable for the way they treat their wives and lead their households. Because I meet with them so often, I am well aware of how well things are going in the home. We all know they must answer to God for their actions. As a spiritual father, I just speak into their lives directly and honestly to help them give a good account to Him.

These men have given me the liberty to identify areas in their life that need spiritual development, and like a coach with his athletes, the combination of correction and exhortation takes them to a new level of ability. The entire family benefits from the G-MEN strategy. While the ministry is directed at men, it is for the benefit of women and children.

MEASURABLE FRUIT

If all I did was meet with my twelve men and have Bible studies, we'd be no more than a fraternity. That's the problem with many cell groups today. I give my men a task that requires them to *apply* the Biblical truths I have been teaching them, so I can know if they are catching on. It's like a drill, spelling test, or work assignment.

"Therefore by *their fruits* you will know them."[12] To know the heart of my men, they must be given the mandate to bear fruit. I can know a man's heart by what he produces. His fruit is a measuring stick. It lets me understand who needs more explanation or help, because faith without works is dead.

At PowerHouse, our measuring stick is our home groups. Every man I mentor must agree to run a home group. Why? Because if he cannot help me minister to the men, women and children in the Body whom we've just won to the Lord, then I'm wasting my time.

We need men who are willing to help cinch the net and chase after the "one sheep that leaves the ninety-nine."[13] I train up leaders to train up leaders. While I am the pastor of every member in my congregation, I cannot possibly give the individual care, attention and ministry that every single member deserves. Men in the mentoring program, along with their wives if they're married, serve as an extension of the ministry to the flock through home groups. This is only possible because I have taken the time to develop the same heart and vision God gave me in twelve other men.

What is Jesus interested in building? The Church.[14] And what is the Church? It's people.

As healthy organisms grow and reproduce, so a healthy church grows and reproduces. As I concentrate on getting a few members truly healthy, the attendance numbers increase without effort. For my "disciples" to help build the church, they have to help build the people.

Relationships are what form the net that keeps people in church long enough to be discipled. We all have to be willing to cultivate relationships within the Body to keep the net intact.

As my twelve men serve as home group leaders, they have an ideal outlet to apply the leadership and ministry principles they learn each week. If their home group is growing, flourishing and functioning as the evangelistic tool it is intended to be, then I can see they understood and applied what we studied. But if a home group is not increasing and growing as it should be, then I can help the leader identify reasons why and help make proper adjustments. People do not do what you *expect* but what you *inspect*. I stay updated and aware of their progress.

The G-MEN strategy is not a religious program. It takes men from *hearing* the Word to being a *doer* of the Word. The entire church benefits. Our strategy establishes relationships that keep converts and members planted in the house. Plus, our spiritual unemployment rate is very low. Every member has an open door to do the work of an evangelist and we are fulfilling all three steps of our church purpose—win, disciple, send.

As a pastor, I've become more of a *spiritual coach*. I raise up *leaders* to raise up *leaders*. The G-MEN strategy is the most effective way to do that.

Todd didn't want to have anything to do with mentoring when we started. He finally agreed but became offended when his mentor, Ken, told him some truth in love. It took everything in Todd to continue on, but he did it. Today Todd and Amy are some of the most productive members of the church. Innovative soul-winners, they are models of true Christianity. I'll just tell you one story about them.

Recently they loaded up the church bus and took sixteen home group members to a nearby area to minister. Todd handed out pens and paper so his team could write down names, addresses and telephone numbers of everyone they met for follow-up purposes. They also took eighty bags of groceries to feed the poor, and he made flyers with the times listed that our bus would be in the area for church pick-ups on Sundays and Wednesdays.

At their first stop, two people were saved. At the next, they led four people to Christ, and had one rededicate her life to the Lord. A crack addict asked for prayer, and they prayed for him. They came to a new area where they'd never been before and fanned out to deliver food. His group ministered to thirty-eight people with four giving their hearts to Christ. Then, eleven people joined hands and prayed for salvation on a single porch. Three generations prayed the sinner's prayer together. The group was overjoyed. But then they bumped into a woman with whom they'd prayed on a previous trip who had been addicted to crack. She was now drug-free and working full-time. They were on a roll ....

As they were leaving, the team still had three bags of food. Spotting three men and a woman sitting around drinking beer, Todd asked if he could pray with them. They said, "We're drinking right now so we don't think it's appropriate." He told them his group wasn't there to condemn them or look down on them. All three gave their lives to Jesus right there.

Dr. Cole says, "The characteristics of a kingdom emanate from the character of the king." This principle applies to a home group leader and its members, as well as a father to his family. Todd's home group did what they had seen him do. Todd did what he had seen his mentor do. God has added men to Todd's mentoring group without him even asking anyone to join. They ask him to be their spiritual father in their quest to become G-MEN.

1 Mark 16:15
2 I Corinthians 14:40
3 Malachi 4:6
4 Proverbs 16:25
5 Hebrews 5:12-14
6 I Corinthians 4:14-15
7 Proverbs 23:7
8 Proverbs 11:14
9 Matthew 10:1
10 John 14:12
11 Hebrews 6:14
12 Matthew 7:20
13 Matthew 18:12
14 Matthew 16:18

7

A MODEL FOR SUCCESS

Men who are "maximized" in their manhood take responsibility for the world around them, showing the love of Christ in a tangible way. Take for example the report I received from one of our mentored men about his mentoring group:

> I want to give you an update on where my group is in the mentoring process. I started mentoring five men of my own about four months ago. We meet at 6 p.m. on Tuesdays at a local restaurant. We met a man who was recently released from prison and invited him and his family to church. He was able to attend his first few weeks out of prison.
>
> His parole officer would only let him work between 6 a.m. and 6 p.m. and wouldn't allow him to go to church again, or to a home group. So, we moved our mentoring meeting from the restaurant to his home. He is growing stronger in the Lord every day. He is learning to be a maximized man. He realizes the only way he can make it after being in prison for so many years is to become a man the way God says it should be done, according to His Word.

Reports like that warm a leader's heart, and let us know we're on track. It works. It's easy to duplicate. It's flexible enough to meet individual needs. Here's the rationale behind what we started:

Objective: *Increase the fish population (Kingdom of God)*

Strategy: *The faster fish mature, the faster they are released to reproduce, which increases the population (Kingdom of God)*

Need: *A system to populate and expedite the maturation process of the believer (fish)*

Now, here's the G-MEN strategy, from A to Z:

Step One: Baby Fish

This is the very first step in the life of a believer. They have just gotten saved and are now a baby Christian. Like a small fish tossed around in the massive ocean, they will have a hard time staying on track if they do not grow bigger (mature in the Word). Like these struggling babies, many new converts never find their way back to the church.

Step Two: The Big Fish

Mark 4:15 tells us the devil comes immediately to steal the Word so the minute a person gets saved, the devil moves in to attack. Once you are born again, you gain a friend in Jesus, but you also attract an enemy—the devil!

Step Three: The Net

The church gathers the converts and like a net rescuing a baby fish, it draws new believers away from the devil and the traps of the world into a spiritual covering of safety.

Step Four: The Nursery

Once converts are in the church, it's time to start maturing them. The home group is like a nursery that helps to nurture them to maturity and the mentoring system is like the food that supplies the strength home groups need to survive and produce other fish (believers)!

Step Five: Sea of Humanity

Once converts are matured into disciples, it is time to send them out into the sea of humanity, the harvest, to start reproducing and making more converts!

The life cycle of the believer does not just happen naturally. A plan must be in place to walk the new convert through to spiritual adulthood. Leaving the fish illustration behind, here's the steps we take with new people, in practical terms.

The New Convert's Track

Step One

When I invite men and women to come to the altar for salvation, our altar workers are our home group leaders. One stands behind each person who responds to the altar call. We pair up women with women and men with men.

Step Two

After we pray, I dismiss the converts and altar ministers into the counseling room. The head altar minister greets the new converts and reiterates the benefits of the decision they just made. After that, altar ministers introduce themselves personally to the person with whom they were paired at the altar. Both the altar minister and the convert fill out an information card that includes their name and phone number. They trade cards. Then the altar worker gives the new convert a direct contact to call for assistance or prayer. The altar minister then prays with him or her for any specific prayer requests they have.

Step Three

The home group system is the secret to retaining new converts. After the prayer, the altar minister walks with the convert to an Information Booth where they are assigned to a home group. Our goal is to plug every new convert into the home group system, since relationship is the number one factor that keeps people coming to church. If they do not attend a home group, or have a relationship with a home group, we assign them to the closest group geographically. If their altar minister's home group is relatively close to them, the convert is assigned to their home group since they now have relationship. Converts are given a flyer with directions and information about their home group. A master list is made to indicate which home group each convert was assigned to.

Step Four

The altar ministers then call each home group leader before 3:00 p.m. that same day and notify them that a new convert has been added to their group. We call this the "hand-off" because the responsibility of keeping track of the convert has now gone from the altar minister to the home group leader.

Step Five

The home group leader calls the new convert assigned to his or her group and personally invites them to attend that evening. They offer transportation and make arrangements to pick that person up if need be. If the convert says they will not be coming, the home group leader reiterates the importance of home groups and explains exactly what takes place during the meetings.

Step Six

The home group leader calls the convert again before Wednesday of the next week to thank them for coming to home group or to invite them again. At the end of the week, the head altar minister calls all the home group leaders assigned new converts to document the results of their phone calls and keep track of converts.

Step Seven

After four weeks, the head altar minister calls the home group leader again to check on the progress of the convert. We are determined to be good stewards of every new soul the Lord sends us and it is worth the extra work to us to have each convert accounted for. This is our "cinch the net" process.

THE VISITOR'S TRACK

We have an entirely different track for visitors who attend church but don't respond to the altar call. If they're in our territory, the battle for their salvation is ours!

Step One

We give all visitors a visitor packet that includes general information about our church, as well as a Visitor Form. We collect completed Visitor Forms in the offering buckets during the first half of our service.

Step Two

Each visitor is placed into a home group before the service is over. If the visitor specifies that they already have a relationship with a home group leader, that is the group they get. Also, if they came with a family member or friend, we assign them to that person's home group leader. Relationship is always the most important factor to consider. If the visitor does not specify an existing relationship, we place them in the home group closest to their home address.

Step Three

All home group leaders check the Information Booth after service. If a visitor has been assigned to their group, the leader is given a box of cookies, along with map directions to the visitor's home. They call the visitors that same day and invite them to home group.

Step Four

The home group leaders take the cookies to visitors' homes to thank them for visiting and invite them to home group. We call this a cookie visit. Home group leaders may choose to delegate cookie visits to another member of their home group. By Tuesday of the following week, the cookie visits are all complete. Whoever does the cookie visit then mails a post card to the visitor the following week to thank them for coming. This personal touch extends the warmth of our ministry. Cookie visits work!

Step Five

All of the information on their Visitor Form is entered into our database.

We are also instituting a visitor reception room so the home group leaders and I can meet the visitors. It's just one more personal touch. The flow chart on the following page will show you the same, and help explain this process:

New Convert/Visitor Track

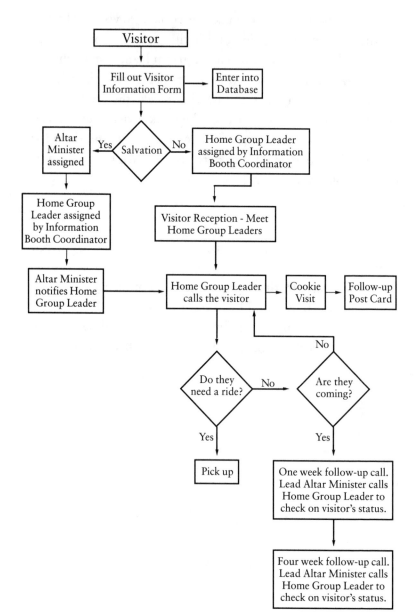

ENCOUNTERS

Like most leaders, I constantly read, ask questions and pray about ways to bring baby Christians to maturity. I focused for some time on discipleship techniques because I recognized that by minimizing the gap of time between the born-again experience and spiritual maturity, we run less risk of losing people back to the world. The verse of Scripture, "My people are destroyed for lack of knowledge,"[1] is a call for leaders to take converts into the knowledge of God as quickly as possible.

Pastor Cesar Castellanos in Bogota, Columbia, John Hagee in San Antonio, Texas and Larry Stockstill in Bakers, Louisiana have all had tremendous success with encounters. Pastor Rocky Malloy implemented this strategy at his church in Santa Cruz, Bolivia and his results alone spurred me to try it.

The anointing breaks the yoke. To impart the anointing, encounters are a tremendous method. During the "encounter," converts are taken to a scenic place to stay for a weekend, away from the cares of everyday life. During those couple of days, they are inundated with the Word. From the time they get up in the morning to the time they go to bed, a trained minister walks them through Biblical truths to bring deliverance and healing to them.

Encounters are a time of repentance and renewal in the Word. Converts come home ready to pursue growth in Christ. The weekend encounter gives the new believer knowledge that might otherwise have taken several months, or even years, for them to learn. It is a great step towards eradicating the ignorance that causes "baby Christians" to head back into the world.

Those are the methods for beginning. Now, how do we get men into mentoring groups, and how do we get them mentoring others?

[1] Hosea 4:6

8

FLOURISHING HOME GROUPS

Jim and Irene were going through some challenges. Jim had some deep questions about doctrinal issues and wanted answers. Irene, though longer in the Lord than Jim, could not answer him to his satisfaction. The situation was creating confusion and tension in the home.

Jim and Irene's home group leaders went to their house one night after home group and took the time to explain Biblical principles and doctrine to Jim. His confusion and uncertainty left and he became empowered by the Holy Spirit as never before. Jim and Irene's hearts were touched that their home group leaders were willing just to sit with them, answer questions and minister to them one on one. They are grateful today for the home group and mentoring strategies.

Ron's home group had been praying over several serious health needs for some time. He wrote me a simple praise report to tell me that his father was healed of liver cancer, another group member's brother was healed of cancer and yet another group member's mother was healed of cancer. Ron said no one could ever convince the men and women in his home group that God doesn't heal the sick!

Let's take a closer look at how the mentoring system works in conjunction with home groups by looking at the chart on the following page:

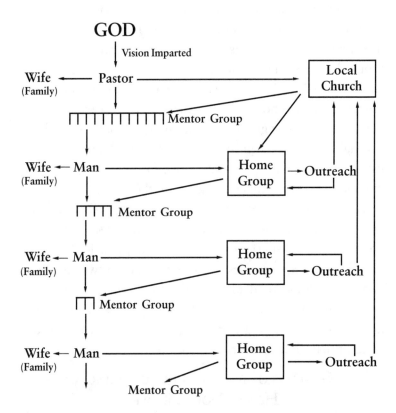

Home groups are multiplication groups. When a group has more than twelve adults, they reproduce, spinning another group off theirs. As a result, home group leaders constantly prepare men from their mentoring group to run a home group. Home group leaders evangelize to grow their group and simultaneously train up husbands and wives as home group leaders. Every time a group needs to multiply, a couple is ready to take it.

Men are given double-duty, because their primary objective is to mentor other men. "Freely you have received, freely give."[1] Men are responsible to minister to their family first and foremost, then a home group, and to look for men in their home group to mentor. They give the men they mentor the same directive—minister to your family, raise up a home group, look for men to mentor.

Once a G-MAN reaches twelve men to mentor, and all twelve are functioning as home group leaders, he is released from running his own home group. At that point, he continues to have oversight of the home groups that his men lead, but he doesn't use his home. That's a great incentive for the leader to get his mentored men fully functioning within the Body.

Also, if one of the mentor's men is mentoring twelve men who are all running a home group, that mentor too can step back from home group leadership and monitor the home group leaders under him. This strategy provides incentive to raise up twelve men as home group leaders and it keeps home groups under authority.

Most importantly, the G-MEN strategy re-emphasizes what is important. Running a home group can be a temporary commitment, but mentoring is for life.

BENEFITS OF MENTORS FUNCTIONING AS HOME GROUP LEADERS

A huge benefit of mentored men leading home groups is to measure fruit. The man's ability to grow a home group successfully tells me he is grasping the spiritual principles taught every week. (Remember—Everything God's involved in multiplies!) But there are more advantages for the G-MEN strategy which runs the mentoring strategy in conjunction with home group leadership.

1. *We inspect and monitor every single home group.*

We have 45 home groups every Sunday night, and are consistently increasing. As a pastor, I could only visit one per week, taking almost a year to visit each home group. It would be close to impossible to identify areas that needed improvement, or take the time to work with each individual home group leader to make changes and consistently monitor their group to make sure progress is being made. However, with the mentoring strategy, I can rest assured that every group is checked regularly. In a single day, I can get an account from my mentored men as to how each and every group is doing. It's much easier to monitor my twelve G-MEN than forty-five home group leaders.

2. *We express gratitude on a regular basis.*

When men and women make the sacrifice of opening up their home every week to lead a home group, they can "grow weary in well doing."[2] But the individual attention my mentors are able to give to the home group leaders prevents burnout and allows us to communicate our gratitude on a personal level on a regular basis.

3. *Counseling needs can be delegated.*

One of the more challenging aspects of tending to the flock is meeting the counseling needs of a congregation. If we're not careful, leaders can find themselves spending most of their workdays behind closed doors giving out advice to one member after another, leaving little time for responsibilities that need attention.

One way to cut back is to minimize the amount of members needing counsel. We accomplish that by teaching men to be the priest and problem-solver of the home. Another effective means is the G-MEN home group leadership structure.

When men and women have counseling needs, they are directed to their home group leader. If their home group leader cannot adequately counsel the need, he tells his mentor. If that mentor sees that I need to be involved, then very quickly and discreetly, that news travels up the mentoring chain to me. At that point, I can choose to meet with the person, or use the opportunity to train someone down the mentoring chain about counseling that specific need.

Most of the counseling needs in my church are handled without me getting involved. That frees me to seek God and do His bidding, while the congregation is still being given sound Biblical counsel. I have confidence they are giving the same advice I would because we've all studied the same principles with our CMN "Majoring In Men" mentoring curriculum.

All we've done is put into process what the Word of God says. "Wherefore, brethren, look ye out among you seven men of honest report, full of the Holy Ghost and wisdom, whom we may appoint over this business. But we will give ourselves continually to prayer, and to the ministry of the word."[3]

G-MEN in the mentoring strategy take responsibility for a portion of the flock through home group leadership. That frees the pastor from working harder to working smarter. He spends more time in the Word and prayer, getting direction and vision from God.

4. *Effective communication lines open.*

Another major benefit of combining mentoring with home group leadership is that I am able to communicate with the congregation effectively and quickly. For example, if we have a church picnic planned for that afternoon, but we need to cancel it due to weather conditions, I can inform the entire church in less than an hour. All I have to do is tell my twelve G-MEN, who call their home group members and G-MEN, who in turn notify the families in their home groups. It really is that simple.

The same thing happens when congregation members have needs. We never have a member in crisis without our leadership knowing.

IDENTIFYING A *SUCCESSFUL* HOME GROUP LEADER

To measure the success of a home group, we needed a way to evaluate both the husband and wife as home group leaders. Her role is crucial. Together they make a complete ministry team. The following home group leadership guidelines apply to both the husband and his wife and were adapted from the book.

TEN CHARACTERISTICS OF A SUCCESSFUL HOME GROUP LEADER[4]

1. *He must love the vision.*

Since there cannot be fruit without love,[5] the vision of home groups must be established in our heart. A good home group leader will live and breathe the vision. He will take ownership of it and do all he can to bring it to pass.

2. *He must not turn away or be distracted from the vision.*

Home group leaders do not allow the group to become stagnant or complacent. Home groups are the backbone of the church, so there cannot be more than one vision. That is called division and a house divided will never stand.[6] A good home group leader does not deviate or depart from the vision.

3. He must not allow his home group to be unfruitful.

A good home group leader is busy evangelizing and multiplying himself. Prayer and fasting are the keys to maintaining a fruitful group.

4. He must be aware of his members' needs throughout the week.

Home groups provide the personal touch that church members need. A good leader makes calls during the week and stays aware of the state of his flock. He arranges for meals to be prepared when a member is sick and he prays with that person daily until they recover. If a woman has a baby, he and his wife visit her. They are caregivers, seven days a week.

5. He will use the home group to restore families.

Home groups focused on ministering the Word of God are the answer to family problems. A good home group leader provides Biblical solutions to the areas of dysfunction a family is experiencing. He consistently works with the families in his group to bring restoration, healing and wholeness to their family relationships.

6. He will make each group member a leader.

Another key to a successful home group is allowing every single member to contribute and function as a leader. A good home group leader works to develop and cultivate leadership skills and attributes in his members. He delegates a portion of the responsibilities that come with running a home group to the group members, so they can grow from that experience.

7. *He will use the home group to promote holiness.*

The accountability that home groups provide provokes members to live a holy life. The group gives them an outlet to confess and abandon their sin, not hide it. The home group leader also provides a model of holiness and sets an upright example for his group.

8. *He will not work on another's ground.*

Home group leaders search for un-churched and un-saved people, not trying to take people out of other churches. People who already go to church are not the targeted group. While they are more than welcome to come to home groups, our emphasis remains on those in need of a shepherd.

9. *He will never allow murmuring, complaining or gossip.*

A home group leader immediately squashes any negative conversation about pastors, leadership or other church members. Gossip is absolutely forbidden in the cell groups and as a result, members leave meetings feeling exhorted and edified, not depressed and discouraged.

10. *He will be faithful in achieving goals.*

A good home group leader sets goals based on evangelism and growth and he applies the Word to see those goals come to pass. Multiplication is always a goal. Since constant growth means constant change, and most people do not like change, the home group leader works to keep his group excited and looking forward to multiplication.

When we take the time to minister to our members on a personal level, we keep people planted in the House, which is essential to spiritual growth. When this list is carried out by the home group leader, that group is going to grow and flourish. Solid relationships, established through the mentoring system, drive people to be willing for this type of *over and above* task.

A Practical Application

Let's walk through how the G-MEN strategy applies to a visitor who comes to our church.

Thursday

Tony's co-worker has been inviting him to church for several weeks. Tony hasn't had the best experience with churches in the past so he is hesitant to bring his family, but he knows he's got to do something. His marriage is not as strong as it used to be and his fourteen-year-old son is acting rebellious. Tony has heard from his co-worker that PowerHouse is "not your average church." He sees the PowerHouse bandit sign at the intersection by his neighborhood, and decides to give it a try.

Friday

Tony tells his co-worker he will come to church on Sunday and they agree to meet in the lobby.

Sunday a.m.

Tony arrives on time with his wife, Marianne, and their children. He is nervous as he approaches the doors of the church. As he enters, his family is greeted with a hug from a smiling member who tells them, "We're so glad you came to the House of God today." He is touched by the friendliness and is even more pleased to see his friend from work waiting for him.

An usher gives Tony and Marianne a Visitor Information packet and shows them to their seats. He's only been sitting down for a matter of seconds when he notices the unusual mix of races. He also can't help but notice that a lot of men attend, which was not the case in the church of his childhood.

Tony and Marianne fill out the Visitor Information Form and place it in the offering plate as it goes by. As the service progresses, they enjoy the upbeat praise and worship and are touched by the message. Tony and Marianne respond to the invitation to rededicate their lives to Christ. They stand together at the altar.

From the altar, they are dismissed into the counseling room where they pray with an altar minister, who is a home group leader, and exchange phone numbers. Tony and Marianne are escorted to the Information Booth and given a flyer with directions to their home group. They are assigned to the same group that Tony's co-worker attends.

Sunday p.m.

Tony receives a phone call from his assigned home group leader, Matt. Matt invites him and his family to home group and Tony agrees to go. He knows this is really out of his comfort zone, but he is curious to see what goes on during a home group meeting. Besides, his friend from work will be there, too.

Tony and Marianne attend home group and are comforted to find they are not the only ones with questions about the Word of God. It is refreshing to hear what Matt and his wife have to say about the pastor's message. Tony likes the fact that everyone is interested in his perspective on the service as well. As Tony and Marianne go to bed that night, they are amazed at the relationships they have formed and new friends they have made in just one day.

Monday, Week Two

Matt and his wife stop by Tony and Marianne's to bring them cookies. They remind Tony and Marianne about the 7:00 p.m. service on Wednesdays. They thank them for coming to home group and pray with them before they leave.

Wednesday, Week Two

Tony and Marianne attend church and their son attends youth group.

Friday, Week Three

Tony and Marianne go out of town for an encounter. They are inundated with the Word and sort through a lot of issues that were hindrances to their faith. They come home refreshed Saturday night with a new zeal and joy in Christ.

Sunday, Week Four

Tony and his family have been coming to church and attending home group for one month now. They also attend adult Sunday School classes on Sunday mornings. Matt asks Tony if he would be interested in joining his mentoring group and Tony agrees to come to a mentoring meeting.

Tuesday, Week Four

Tony attends mentoring and realizes there is an entirely different level of discipleship that he needs. He is amazed at the amount of revelation the curriculum has to offer and he can't wait to start applying the truths he is hearing to his own marriage.

Month Two

Tony has been coming to mentoring and he is now really starting to grasp the vision of the church. His mentor, Matt, helped him and Marianne to get involved with the Children's Ministry. They have now made significant friendships within the church. They are studying the mentoring curriculum together in the evenings and Marianne has a renewed sense of hope for their marriage. Tony is also learning how to minister to his son and their relationship is mending.

Month Six

Tony and Marianne have gone on several outreaches with their home group and have caught on to soul winning. They have done cookie visits and often help Matt with phone calls during the week to other home group members. Tony and Marianne have brought friends and family to church and they too are now being transformed by the Gospel.

Matt talks to Tony and Marianne about running their own home group. They have been faithful to church, adult Sunday School, home groups and mentoring. Tony and Marianne pray about it. They finally decide they would like to open their home and serve as home group leaders.

Month Eight

Tony and Marianne have been running a home group for two months and Tony has two men that are interested in mentoring. Tony starts holding mentoring meetings with them once a week.

Month Ten

Three more men come to Tony's mentoring group and his home group flourishes. Tony's marriage has been transformed and communication with his son is now healthy and meaningful. Tony and Marianne are counseling a couple in their home group who are having marital problems.

One Year Later

Tony has seven men in his mentoring group and two of them lead home groups of their own. Tony's home is in order and his family has become a major source of support and strength in the church. Tony's home group has multiplied twice now and his home group members are learning what it means to fulfill the Great Commission. Tony and Marianne have helped facilitate an encounter and they are still a great help in the Children's Ministry.

Implementation Plan

When it comes to implementing the G-MEN strategy, it's not easy to determine where to start. The first variable to consider is, do you currently have home groups in place?

If the answer is YES:

The pastor chooses his twelve strongest home group leaders and starts mentoring them. If there happens to be men in the church who possess the kind of leadership the pastor needs in his G-MEN group, but they do not lead a home group, they must be willing to start facilitating a home group. Remember, if a man is not willing to help minister to the rest of the flock, the pastor will not benefit personally from pouring his life into that man.

Once the pastor has identified twelve men, the rest of the home group leaders are divided up into groups of twelve and placed under the twelve men. The pastor's G-MEN mentor the rest of the home group leaders and help them to run their home group in the most efficient and effective way possible.

Men mentored by the pastor, whom we'll call Generation A and those mentored by the pastor's G-Men, whom we'll call Generation B, look for men in their home groups to mentor and raise up as home group leaders. The mentoring process births generations C, D, and so on.

If the answer is NO (that your church currently doesn't operate by cells):

The pastor chooses his twelve strongest leaders and starts mentoring them using the "Majoring in Men" curriculum. They do their lessons with their families at home, to mentor their homes.

Once the mentoring process has started, the men start home groups with their wives to accommodate the entire congregation. If the congregation is too large, they start mentoring other leaders who will lead home groups as well. Many variables go into such plans.

The beauty of the strategy is its flexibility. In fact, the G-MEN strategy *must* be adjusted and customized to accommodate each individual church and culture. Pastor Kong Hee divided his city into quadrants and teaches all the men from the various quadrants on a monthly basis. Bishop Eddie Long teaches his men as a whole every Saturday.

I have determined to make myself available to every leader who reads this book to help develop your strategy. My contact information and pledge to this effect is in the "epilogue" of this book. I encourage you to link arms with us. Let's work together to make the G-MEN strategy a reality in your group, congregation or community!

[1] Matthew 10:8
[2] Galatians 6:9
[3] Acts 6:3
[4] Rocky Malloy, G-12, Unpublished, Galveston, TX, page 119
[5] Colossians 3:14
[6] Matthew 12:25

9

Two Kinds of Administration

Two types of church government exist: the Rake and the Wheel.

In rake administration, the head leads from above and all work is initiated, propelled and inspected by him. The prongs—staff and leadership—hang on for the ride and do not assume ownership of the ministry.

At the end of the rake comes dirt because prongs don't produce fruit. The pastor must pull the prongs where his vision is taking him.

In wheel administration, the leader is like the hub in the middle and leadership is like spokes coming out. Everyone is connected to the hub, which is their source of vision.

The pastor duplicates himself so the leadership can support a portion of the ministry, which is the outer ring. All the spokes are connected and joined together through relationship and all bear equal parts of the load. Their ability to work together determines how fast the wheel can roll.

It Starts With the Leader

The same way men are called to be responsible for their wives, I am called, as a pastor, to be responsible for the congregation. No program in the church works without the visionary connected to it. Cell groups fail if a pastor only implements the program people want, with no vision or heart for it. Leaders cannot delegate the mentoring process to a men's minister and expect great results with no personal involvement. The pastor must take an active role in mentoring men, which is the beginning of the restoration process of the church. *He is the chief of the fathers*[1] and sets an example of fatherhood. He can't just teach it from the pulpit.

If the cell groups in my church are not working, it's not a member or leader's fault. I delegate a large part of our ministry efforts to men and women, but I have to take personal responsibility for the condition of the flock. Along with the authority of being a pastor comes the accountability for ministry. Dr. Cole says, "Mediocre men want authority without accountability." The pastor is the driving force and must be willing to take responsibility for overall implementation.

We cannot be out to get glory for ourselves. We just pour ourselves into others and by giving, we will receive. If we're always worried about who's going to get the glory we deserve, or who is going to rise up and back stab us, then we have forgotten that promotion comes from God.

"Except the Lord build the house, they labour in vain that build it."[2] Anything man tries to accomplish in the Kingdom of God that the Lord does not support, will fail. So, if we're concerned about Judas rising up to destroy us, we must understand that Judas did not have the power to destroy

Jesus. Judas paved the way to get Jesus to the Cross, which was His place of victory.

We can have dictatorship or we can have duplication. With duplication, we'll leave a legacy that will continue to bring glory to God even after we're gone. We have to be willing to give up doing everything ourselves so that everything will get done. We need to train up our spiritual sons so they can have their own someday.

Every leader must decide which type of administration he or she will follow—the rake of the dictator or the wheel of the duplicator. We have to be willing to pour ourselves into other faithful men and women—for a lifetime.

A mentoring member named Doug wrote me this report:

> *After the men in your mentoring group spoke at the men's breakfast this Saturday, I heard men commenting on how much they sound like you. I explained that when you meet with your men every week, you impart into them and that is the power of the structure we have in place at our church. You are duplicating yourself in them.*
>
> *One of the men I have been mentoring for ten weeks facilitated our home group this past weekend. When the meeting was over, people were commenting that he sounded just like me.*
>
> *Both of these instances are proof that the duplication process is taking place. As you know, I am mentored by Terry from your group. Terry sounds like you, I sound like you and the men I mentor are starting to sound like you because we are all linked together through mentoring which uses the CMN curriculum. We are all focused on the same vision and we're all becoming more Christlike. I'm excited to be here in this church for this!*

MYTHS ABOUT SMALL GROUPS

Myth #1 – The families in my church don't need or want home group meetings.

On Sunday mornings, the church is full of smiling members. Men lovingly place their arms around wives' shoulders and children look content as they sit with their parents during service. One glance around the sanctuary and it appears to be full of happy, loving families. The truth is, a man can be kind to his wife at church, even if they are not speaking at home. Children can sit by their parents and still be full of anger and frustration.

People may be able to fake it at church, but when the church meets in the home, it's a different story. Sooner or later, in a small group setting, dysfunctional situations will surface. All that can be hidden in a traditional church service are not so easy to conceal when you are asked to share with the rest of the group. So, if a person does not like the idea of cells, they should examine themselves and ask why.

In a book entitled *G-12*, Rev. Rocky Malloy addresses this topic. "How many times have couples divorced and no one knew they were having problems? I'm not just talking about the wallpaper couples in the church. I'm talking about the pastors, deacons and elders. Their colleagues knew nothing about it until the divorce. Unless you are in peoples' homes regularly, you don't know what is going on in their lives. Small groups are good because they hold us accountable."[3]

The small group relationship worked well for Jesus because He had nothing to hide. As a matter of fact, it helped to prove that He was sinless. When we allow people to get close to us, we show them our character. As Rev. Malloy points out, a jury of twelve peers choose guilt or innocence for people on trial. It's the same for leaders. When the vast numbers of people know we have a "jury of twelve" who are up close and still say we're okay, they believe we're probably okay. Having people close to us keeps leaders accountable, as much as we keep them accountable.

Greg's wife had a friend to whom she had been ministering. The friend's husband wanted nothing to do with the things of God and the woman left him. She said she just couldn't take it anymore. One night Greg received a phone call from this woman's husband. He said his marriage was over and he felt like his life had hit rock bottom. His wife had told him to call Greg because she knew he and his wife ran a home group and had experience working with couples.

Greg listened to the man, and realized he needed Jesus and the truth of God's Word. Although Greg was too busy to meet with him privately right away, to keep from putting the man off, he invited him to sit in on his mentoring meeting that week. Greg figured the principles they talk about would be exactly what he needed to hear.

The man came and could not believe what he heard. He wanted what Greg and the other men had. He knew in his heart what he had to do, and right there, he gave his life to the Lord.

We never know what people are experiencing or needing. Having a strategy in place with a structure enables us to meet the needs of every individual.

Myth #2 – The small group setting makes people uncomfortable.

The home group setting does require men and women to trust others with their emotions, which is not easy for most people. They are afraid they'll be taken advantage of or manipulated. The thought of exposing certain areas of their lives scares them. Confessing our sins in private to God gets us forgiven.[4] Confessing our sins one to another, makes us whole through accountability![5] But, planting themselves in a home group conquers all their fear as they realize they are not the only ones with struggles and imperfections. The love an individual receives from home groups eventually replaces all fear. People develop a renewed sense of confidence as they grow in relationship with other believers.

On two successive Sundays, one of our home groups led by Ken and Lori experienced amazing answers to prayer. On one night, they received a phone call from a man asking if they still had that "home group thing" going on. Ken informed him that they were actually right in the middle of home group and they would love to have him join them. The man hesitated, stating he didn't want to bother them with his problems and he hung up the phone. The home group immediately began praying for this man in earnest. The next Sunday, he showed up in church and gave his life to Jesus.

A woman was coming regularly to Ken and Lori's home group but her husband would not come. The next Sunday night after this miraculous salvation, that husband showed up in the middle of their home group and, with tears in his eyes, he embraced his wife and told her he felt he just had to come.

Far from creating discomfort, God heals families and the prayers of our home groups make a difference!

Myth #3 – Home groups provide ample circumstances for a church split.

The truth is, cell groups provide the relationships that prevent revolt. If a wolf should surface, he can only take a single small group with him, not the whole church. The organization of small groups protects against splits. If a split were to occur, the losses are minimal.

Rev. Malloy says, "What is more devastating? Losing 90% of the people through the back door or 10% through a split?"[6] We certainly lose more people out the back door by not meeting their needs than by church splits.

Home groups actually benefited me as a pastor in a unique way. Suddenly, people I'd known for years received a unique perspective on church and leadership.

For one thing, they became convicted about church attendance. They'd call their list during the week and invite people, who said they would come. They'd study their home group notes and get the message and topic of discussion settled in their spirit and ready for the meeting. They'd clean their house and organize chairs in the living room. They'd pray over the home group meeting and ask God's presence to touch every man, woman and child. Then, 6:00 p.m. would roll around and only 25% of the people showed up. These home group leaders have a new respect for leadership! They realize what a huge commitment it takes every day. Once a week seems like more than enough.

THE BOTTOM LINE

When you get right down to it, what matters more than what the charts and graphs say home groups and mentoring are doing for your church is what the people in your church say it's doing for their lives. I receive literally hundreds of praise reports from my congregation about the miracles God manifests in their lives through home groups and the mentoring system.

Ernie and Debbie planned to take their home group for a neighborhood outreach for months but kept getting rained out. Eventually, on a beautiful Saturday, they were able to canvass the nearby streets. One of the home group members had stapled over 100 packets together that contained a home group flyer, a ladies conference brochure, a "ticket" to church and a Gospel tract.

Nine of the group members left Debbie's and Ernie's house at 10:00 a.m. Everyone was so excited when they finished the first street, that they wanted to do more. On the next street Ernie's teenaged son Daniel led two young men to the Lord. They went to a third street and led two more young men to the Lord.

Ernie and Debbie treated their home group to lunch afterwards and they had a great time. Having a fellowship after such productivity makes everyone feel great. They prayed together and thanked God for every seed sown, trusting God for an overflowing house on Sunday evening.

Regardless of the outcome or growth, that group had already won. They were won, discipled, sent, and produced a harvest for the Kingdom. Rake or wheel—dictator or duplicator—that's what it's all about!

1 Ezra 3:12
2 Psalm 127:1
3 Rocky Malloy, G-12, Unpublished, Galveston, TX
4 I John 1:9
5 James 5:16
6 Rocky Malloy, G-12, Unpublished, Galveston, TX

10

Choosing Your G-Men

Quoting one of my spiritual fathers, Dr. Cole has often said, "God's methods are men. While men look for better methods, God looks for better men."

How should we choose our twelve men? Like Jesus did: one at a time.

As leaders, choosing whom to pour ourselves into is an extremely important decision. It's even more important considering that the rest of the flock will line up under them. We cannot base our decisions on who has been a Christian the longest, who has given the most financial support, or who would be appalled if they were not asked to be in the group. We need to start with twelve men who possess the heart and spirit of a leader.

"Moreover thou shalt provide out of all the people able men, such as fear God, men of truth, hating covetousness; and place such over them, to be rulers of thousands, and rulers of hundreds, rulers of fifties, and rulers of tens: And let them judge the people at all seasons: and it shall be, that every great matter they shall bring unto thee, but every small matter they shall judge: so shall it be easier for thyself, and they shall bear the burden with thee. If thou shalt do this thing, and God command thee so, then thou shalt be able to endure, and all this people shall also go to their place in peace."[1] These are the kinds of men a leader needs to seek. Faithful men, fair and godly men, men of truth. These are real leaders.

I have found it to be true that "some people make things happen, some people watch what happens and some people wonder what happened." The "Majoring in Men" curriculum teaches that leaders determine to influence while followers only happen to influence. If a mentoring strategy is going to work, the leader needs men in his group who are determined to make a difference.

By implementing this strategy, motives are exposed. Men in search of personal recognition will not want to humble themselves under a mentor. Men who are double-minded will not like the accountability mentoring brings. "Good ole' boys" who are only out to impress the pastor tend to shy away from the responsibility of caring for other church members. Men who only "play church" resent the fact that mentoring requires them to bear fruit.

One thing is for sure, the G-MEN strategy "separates the men from the boys." The leader's job is to choose twelve Christlike men, then equip them to be even better leaders, so they can go back and train up the boys.

I like the following anonymous statements about the difference between leaders and followers. They always encourage me.

> *When leaders make a mistake, they say, "I was wrong;" when followers make a mistake, they say, "It wasn't my fault."*

> *A leader works harder than a follower and has more time; a follower is always "too busy" to do what is necessary.*

> *A leader goes through a problem; a follower goes around it and never gets past it.*

A leader makes and keeps commitments;
a follower makes and forgets promises.

A leader says, "I'm good, but not as good as I ought
to be;" a follower says, "I'm not as bad as a
lot of other people."

Leaders listen; followers just wait until it's
their turn to talk.

Leaders respect those who are in authority over them
and try to learn something from them; followers
resent those who are superior to them and
try to find chinks in their armor.

Leaders feel responsible for more than their job;
followers say, "I only work here."

A leader says, "There ought to be a better way to do
this;" followers say, "That's the way it's
always been done here."

WHAT GOD LOOKS FOR IN A LEADER

While we are only able to see a man's outward appearance, God is able to see right into the heart of a man. "But the Lord said unto Samuel, Look not on his countenance, or on the height of his stature; because I have refused him: for the Lord seeth not as man seeth; for man looketh on the outward appearance, but the Lord looketh on the heart."[2]

God is a much better judge of who exactly should be in our group. We must seek God and pray about our decision

100

to recruit men into our mentoring group. We have to be led by the Spirit of God in order to choose the right men. The repercussions of people doing the choosing, is that we tend to choose men like Saul, who are big in stature but small in heart. When the battle comes, men like Saul don't stand for the people or God's cause. The people may have chosen Saul but God chose David.

By examining the character of David, we can identify some attributes that God considers to be leadership qualities.

1. David was faithful –

"And Samuel said to Jesse, 'Are all the young men here?' Then he said, 'There remains yet the youngest, and there he is, keeping the sheep.' "[3] While all of David's brothers were at home, he was out working and watching over the sheep. You need men who are faithful like David. While they could be sitting at home, instead they are at church, every week, year round. "Confidence in an unfaithful man in a time of trouble is like a bad tooth and a foot out of joint."[4] Faithfulness is a must. Dr. Cole says, "You can make a faithful man able but you cannot make an able man faithful."

2. David was committed to the vision –

You cannot afford to choose men who are apathetic toward the vision of your church. You need men who are passionate about the work of the ministry and eager to step up to a greater commitment level. They should cry out like David, "Is there not a cause?"[5] Rather than pointing out why your vision won't work all the time, you need men who take your vision and work it out.

3. David was an overcomer –

You don't want people who tend to give up or turn back when they are challenged. When Saul faced a challenge, he reacted in fear instead of faith. We want men like David who run at the enemy and do not faint in the day of adversity. "And it came to pass, when the Philistine arose, and came and drew nigh to meet David, that David hasted, and ran toward the army to meet the Philistine."[6]

4. David had a good track record –

David had already killed a lion and a bear before he faced Goliath. Choose men of integrity who have already proven to be men of their word. If you have been able to trust them with a little, you know you can trust them with a lot. "Thou hast been faithful over a few things, I will make thee ruler over many things."[7]

5. David possessed a caregiver's heart –

"And David said unto Saul, Thy servant kept his father's sheep, and there came a lion, and a bear, and took a lamb out of the flock: And I went out after him, and smote him, and delivered it out of his mouth: and when he arose against me, I caught him by his beard, and smote him, and slew him."[8] David risked his life to save the sheep. The men you choose for your group are going to be an extension of you to the rest of the flock so they must have a heart to love and care for all types of people.

6. David possessed evidence of his relationship with God –

"David said moreover, The Lord that delivered me out of the paw of the lion, and out of the paw of the bear, he will deliver me out of the hand of this Philistine."[9] It was obvious that David had relationship with God. The men you choose must have evidence that they know God and must possess the character described in 1 Timothy 3:1-13. Men who have relationship with God will be the ones who are always getting people saved, always going above and beyond what they are asked to do to see lives impacted for Christ. Then, when those men duplicate themselves, you will have a lineage of men after God's heart.

7. David was willing to serve –

"And Jesse said unto David his son, Take now for thy brethren an ephah of this parched corn, and these ten loaves, and run to the camp to thy brethren."[10] David possessed a servant's heart. Find men who are willing to sweep, clean toilets and do whatever you ask them to because they love God and recognize you as a leader. Go ahead and try men out by asking them to do things that require a servant's heart. If they do it without hesitation over a period of time (consistency), they are qualifying themselves to be in your group.

8. David had a mindset of victory –

"This day will the Lord deliver thee into mine hand; and I will smite thee, and take thine head from thee; and I will give the carcasses of the host of the Philistines this day unto the fowls of the air, and to the wild beasts of the earth; that all the earth may know that there is a God in Israel."[11] David never doubted that he was going to prevail over the enemy. You need men that are multi-talented, confident in their God and full of faith. Run away from a murmurer or complainer. Put them several lines down the mentoring chain under someone who has overcome in that area, so they can minister to them. Your front line twelve need to be ready for battle. They must be willing to let you cut them and not cry about it or leave the House over it.

THE VALUE OF WORKING WITH LEADERS

"Now when Jesus was in Bethany, in the house of Simon the leper, there came unto him a woman having an alabaster box of very precious ointment, and poured it on his head, as he sat at meat. But when his disciples saw it, they had indignation, saying, To what purpose is this waste? For this ointment might have been sold for much, and given to the poor. When Jesus understood it, he said unto them, Why trouble ye the woman? for she hath wrought a good work upon me. For ye have the poor always with you; but me ye have not always."[12]

The disciples were angry when the woman poured the ointment on Jesus because they perceived that it should have gone to someone poor and more needy than Him. They thought that expensive oil was being wasted.

Leaders often focus the majority of our ministry efforts on those in major need of spiritual maturity and growth. As a result, those who already possess the attributes of a Godly leader are neglected. Being unemployed, they use their job, or other secular outlets to exercise their gifts.

As we redirect our attention to utilize the leaders in our church, some may say, "Why is the pastor spending so much time ministering to men who already live a victorious Christian life when there are so many men who are broken and really need his help?" The truth is, the spiritually poor we will have with us always.

We need to pour ourselves, like the anointing in the alabaster box, into the twelve most qualified leaders we can. Then they can minister to the rest of the people's needs.

"And the things that thou hast heard of me among many witnesses, the same commit thou to faithful men, who shall be able to teach others also."[13] It's never a waste of our time to impart our anointing into the leadership of our church.

MENTORING COVENANTS

The mentoring relationship is not casual, but a covenant relationship. It is for life a pledge to God as well as man. In order to make this more of a reality, we created written mentoring covenants—one for the men who are being mentored to agree to and one for the men who are mentoring men to agree to.

This is what men who desire to be mentored at my church pledge to do:

I, _____, agree to be spiritually
    trained and mentored

by _____ .

I pledge to:

1. Attend all PHCC services, special functions and home group meetings and participate fervently and loyally. In the event that an uncontrollable circumstance occurs that hinders my participation, I will notify my mentor well in advance with the reason. This is accountability and gives honor to God.

2. Complete all curriculum and/or other assignments required of me by my mentor and to turn them in on time.

3. Receive all instruction, and even correction, without allowing myself to be offended. I want to grow and mature in the things of God and I believe that by submitting myself under my mentor, I will be a valuable tool in the arsenal of God at PHCC.

4. Discuss spiritual principles with my wife on a daily basis and to pray with her, as well as my children, every day. I recognize that I am the Priest in my home and I will exercise that authority by ministering to their needs!

5. Begin recruiting other men to mentor. My ultimate goal is to fortify the home group structure, which is the heartbeat of our church.

6. Refuse to murmur—about anything! I desire to be a leader in this move of God because it gives significance to my life, therefore, I will only speak those things which are edifying and exhorting!

7. Live with my priorities in this order:

    1. God and His will
    2. Family
    3. Job

I will change my thinking about my time and God's time— it's all His! When I gave Him my life, my time was included in that commitment!

8. Tithe and offer cheerfully.

This is what every man who mentors agrees to:

As a mentor, I pledge to:

1. Be available
2. Provide support
3. Pray for you daily
4. Give only Word-based counsel
5. Be on time to our meetings
6. Challenge you and keep you accountable to the purpose and vision of God for your life through the vehicle of PHCC
7. Say the hard things when I don't want to
8. Require excellence, consistency and holiness, integrity and Godly character as fruit in your life
9. Evaluate your performance

_____   _____
             Signature   Date

---

[1] Exodus 18:21-23
[2] I Samuel 16:7
[3] I Samuel 16:11
[4] Proverbs 25:19
[5] I Samuel 17:29
[6] I Samuel 17:48
[7] Matthew 25:21
[8] I Samuel 17:34-35
[9] I Samuel 17:37
[10] I Samuel 17:17
[11] I Samuel 17:46
[12] Matthew 26:6-11
[13] II Timothy 2:2

11

MENTORING MEETINGS

O nce you've made the decision about who to bring into your group, one more decision has the potential to "make or break" the mentoring process. You must decide *what* to teach the men.

For me, there is no question as to what would be the best catalyst for spiritual growth after this book. I choose Dr. Cole's curriculum, *Majoring In Men*. Dr. Cole's revelations on godly manhood challenge every man to come up to a new level in Christ. Also, by using curriculum, instead of leaving the topic of meetings up to the mentor's discretion, I can ensure that the same Biblical concepts and principles are being taught all the way down the mentoring chain. By the time the men have completed this curriculum, they have read the following books, all written by Dr. Cole:

- Maximized Manhood
- Courage
- Sexual Integrity
- Potential Principle
- Communication, Sex and Money
- Winners Aren't Those Who Never Fail, But Those Who Never Quit
- Real Men
- Strong Men In Tough Times
- The Unique Woman

Each book is accompanied by thought-provoking worksheets that highlight the main points of each chapter. Every man is required to complete the worksheets with his wife, who is his first disciple. Then we discuss their answers during our mentoring meetings. This mandates quality time to build family relationships around the Word of God and the issues of life.

Every once in a while, when a special event or guest speaker is coming to the church, I may take a week or two off from the curriculum and focus specifically on the event at hand. For example, if I have Brother Hilton Sutton coming in to speak on the book of Revelation, we may spend a mentoring meeting talking about the end times so they are prepared for his teaching.

I like for the expectancy level of the congregation to be at an all-time high when guest ministers come to minister here. I've found that taking time to discuss the gift of God that is about to speak into their lives gets them excited and ready for a Word from God. It makes the most of the five-fold gifts that God gives us favor enough to host. Then, it's easy to get right back on track with the curriculum when the event has passed.

THE COMMISSIONING

Upon completion of the curriculum, men qualify to be commissioned by the Christian Men's Network. The purpose of commissioning men is to entrust men with the message and ministry of Christlike manhood and to launch, establish or support ministry to men. Commissioned men will reach men individually, in their local church, within a region or on a national or international scope. Commissioned men work under the auspices of the local church leadership and are accountable in men's ministry to their pastors and the CMN Board of Directors.

A Ceremony to commission the men is held at the CMN headquarters or it can be held at your church. The men are presented a sword as they commit to the following commission statement:

> *"I am commissioned with a ministry majoring in men, to witness to the men of this generation and bring them to an identification with Christ, impressing them with the reality that 'manhood and Christlikeness are synonymous'."*

MENTORING MEETING AGENDA

1. When?

I meet with my guys at 6:00 a.m. on Wednesdays. I meet with them at that time so that mentoring doesn't take away from their family time.

2. Where?

We usually meet at a restaurant right down the street from the church. The casual setting keeps the men relaxed and they can also eat breakfast if they choose to. I do not stand behind a pulpit or elevate myself. I just sit at the table with them and look them straight in the eyes as we speak to one another.

3. How long?

Meetings usually last an hour to an hour and a half.

4. *What goes on during a meeting?*

While I do not feel the need to stick to one particular meeting agenda every single week, I also feel like having a structure in place helps meetings run smoothly and timely. The following is a general overview of a meeting agenda:

1. *Open up in prayer* – I call on different men to pray every time.

2. *Review mentoring materials* – We discuss the lesson and review the worksheets. I go around the table and get comments from each man. I ask thought-provoking questions and the men share what the Lord spoke to them through the lesson. This process meets their need to be whole and fathered.

3. *Share home group success strategies* – We constantly exchange ideas pertaining to home group growth and the men learn from each other.

4. *Discuss church business* – I keep my men updated on all upcoming events and we talk about where their involvement and support is needed. I give them copies of the staff meeting minutes for that week because I consider them staff.

5. *Prayer requests* – Toward the end of the meeting, I like to go around the group and take any prayer requests the men have so I can be in agreement with them during the week.

6. *Close in prayer* – Once again, each week I pick a different man to close us in prayer.

GET CLOSE!

Besides the mentoring meeting, I attempt to have lunch or quality one-on-one time once or twice a month with each man. During those times, we discuss more personal matters.

There is *nothing* complicated about mentoring! As a matter of fact, there's really nothing difficult about implementing this entire G-MEN strategy. I have found that most leaders have a multitude of questions. That is why we are dedicated to assisting churches that desire to enjoy the same benefits of this strategy we have.

I believe the G-MEN strategy truly is the missing link to revival for the twenty-first century Church.

The G-MEN strategy requires men to get out of their comfort zones in order to live in the blessing zone.

The G-MEN strategy demands organized religion to evaluate its purpose and provides structure in an hour where signs, wonders and miracles are being poured out in great proportions.

The G-MEN strategy crosses denominational, racial and cultural boundaries and directs our attention to one central focus: becoming more like Christ.

The G-MEN strategy challenges us to believe in people, love the unlovable and make disciples out of anyone and everyone who is willing.

The G-MEN strategy provokes men to make a demand on God's Word and to exercise their faith so that natural obstacles become supernatural victories.

The G-MEN strategy uses God's most powerful weapon—believers—to win back His most prized possession—mankind.

The G-MEN strategy is for men who are ready to labor in God's harvest, who are unashamed of the Gospel of Jesus Christ, and ready to take the oath of the fellowship of the unashamed:

FELLOWSHIP OF THE UNASHAMED

I am part of the fellowship of the unashamed.

The die has been cast, the decision has been made.

I have stepped over the line.

I won't look back, let up, slow down, back away, or be still.

My past has been redeemed, my present makes sense and my future is secure.

I'm finished and done with low living, sight walking, small planning, smooth knees, colorless dreams, tame visions, mundane talking, cheap giving and dwarf goals.

I no longer need pre-eminence, promotion, plaudits or popularity.

I don't have to be right, first, tops, recognized, praised, regarded or rewarded.

I now live by faith, I lean on God's presence, I love with patience, live with prayer, labor with power.

My face is set, my gait is fast and my goal is Heaven.

My road is narrow, my way is rough, my companions are few . . . but my guide is reliable and my mission is clear.

I cannot be bought, compromised, detoured, lured away, deluded or delayed.

I will not flinch in the face of sacrifice, hesitate in the presence of adversity, negotiate at the table of the enemy, ponder at the pool of popularity, or meander in the maze of mediocrity.

I won't give up, shut up, let up, or slow up, until I've stayed up, stored up, prayed up, paid up and spoken up for the cause of Christ.

I am a disciple of Jesus.

I must go 'til He comes, give 'til I drop.

12

THE NEED FOR G-MEN

Everywhere I go, no matter what social circle I find myself in, Christian or secular, I ask men the question, "What kind of relationship did you have with your father?" Nine out of ten men say it was less than ideal, if they had one at all. I already listed all of the ills of society that can be traced to a lack of fathers. But we cannot overstate the problem fatherlessness has created around the world. We cannot be nonchalant about the fact that we, the Church, have the answer to the plagues brought about by absentee and apathetic fathers.

After David killed Goliath, Saul asked the ultimate question: "Whose son is he?"[1] Why did he ask this question? Because when you know the father, you know the son.

In Saul's day, a son always worked in his father's business, under his mentoring and instruction. This working relationship cultivated a personal relationship between men and their sons. Communication was an imperative. They co-labored to achieve a common goal—maintaining the family business, which supplied a common need—food and provision.

The attention men gave their sons in those days provided a twofold benefit. Jesse not only taught his son David to be an expert in his occupation, he also imparted character-building qualities like integrity and godliness. David's natural gifts were enhanced, while his character was strengthened. When David was promoted for a job well done, he had enough spiritual insight to handle the success.

Wouldn't it be great if more of our most admired and talented athletes in the world today also had character? Little boys and girls across America have posters hanging in their rooms of people who, in many cases, have an abundance of talent but lack moral character.

All over the world, men now substitute a higher education for a relationship with their father and mentor. The results are that we have a more educated society, but we are more insecure, unloved, unbalanced and unfulfilled than ever. As a result, people search for gratification in pornography, drugs and promiscuity, only to find they've been made a slave to these transgressions.

How much money is spent daily by people trying to quench the void from being unfulfilled? I wonder how many women, just today, went further into debt to buy clothes so they could dress themselves up in an attempt to feel better about themselves? How many young people got a tattoo or pierced their body just so someone would notice them?

Humanity always tries to compensate for emptiness by dressing up the outside. When a girl knows her father loves and values her, she does not feel the need to get attention from men by compromising her body. When a boy has a father who takes the time to speak to him and then listens to what he has to say, he doesn't make wild marks on his body for attention.

In times past, entire families lived on the same property. Each new generation had relationship with their grandparents and even great-grandparents. Today, the family unit is broken and families are scattered all over the country and world. Statistically, 52% of marriages in America fail. Even if a family manages to stay close geographically, divorce divides them emotionally. We offer our children on the altar of divorce and we sever family ties.

It's time for the Church to realize we are a surrogate family, and we must put structure and support back into the world. The mentoring process of the G-MEN strategy creates a surrogate father position in a man's life and provides the love and care he needs to become an overcomer, leader and winner.

Most men seize an opportunity to link themselves up to a man of God who will pour truth into them. It's not that men have not wanted to know the truth about family and life. It's that no one was teaching it.

Universally, the need for godly fathers who care means the G-MEN strategy will work in every society. The G-MEN strategy provides an answer for a very real problem. To reduce abuse and crime, and reverse the curse that Adam brought on us in the Garden of Eden, we must disciple the twenty-first century man into a godly man, a man with the nature and love of God in his heart. Men must comprehend that manhood and Christlikeness are synonymous.

Even Hollywood has picked up on the need for leaders. Movies like Braveheart, the Patriot, and Gladiator center around a heroic man who stands up for what he believes and brings justice to the people.

I do not think trying to reach the culture of our society by thumping a Bible or pointing a religious finger is going to turn the hearts of the people. We must show the love of Christ. We teach people to overcome the thing that most complicates their lives—sin.

The G-MEN strategy is not a religious organization. It is simply a method of duplicating the men who have found the truth and have seen the light of God's Word expose and destroy areas of darkness in their lives. These are men who have been fathered and equipped to take their light into all the world. I call them "curators" of the truth. Jesus is the way, the truth and the life and no man can come to the Father except through Him.[2] We are determined to introduce all of humanity to Jesus—a truth that is consistent and can be counted on every time.

MENTORING OUR YOUTH

"The father of the righteous shall greatly rejoice: and he that begetteth a wise child shall have joy of him. Thy father and thy mother shall be glad, and she that bare thee shall rejoice."[3]

We recognize the need for fathers for our young men. With such tremendous results mentoring the adults, we implemented mentoring for our teenaged congregation as well. We provide mentoring for the young men, as well as the young women, which has taken our young people to an entirely new level.

Teenagers in the mentoring process are learning to take ownership of their youth ministry. They are learning what it means to be a leader. They're getting concentrated doses of the Word. They have a "Mentoring Covenant" specific to the issues of young people and they are committed to being an example of Christ in their home, church and school. We started mentoring our teenagers long after we started mentoring men and families, but already our youth pastors, along with a faithful group of volunteers, mentor over forty young men and women.

Parents and teachers are marveling at the amount of growth, wisdom and maturity they see in the mentored teens. The young people are catching the attention of their parents, the congregation and the community, which builds their esteem and confidence. They are learning how to be holy in the midst of a wicked generation, how to overcome negative peer pressure with the Word of God. Their mentors are training them up to lead small groups that meet every Sunday evening.

Many of the young people in our mentoring system have parents that are not saved or serving God. However, we're setting the example of Christ for them and we're teaching them how to win their parents to the Lord. G-MEN are acting as surrogate fathers to the young men and women who do not have fathers in their home. We're showing them how to stop the curse of fatherlessness that has plagued their families and they are learning how to make wise decisions that will someday lead to a healthy marriage and family of their own.

Dr. Cole has developed a powerful curriculum for teens entitled "Majoring in Young Men." It's provided the perfect study guide. We're able to adapt the curriculum and use a majority of the material for our young ladies as well. Having teenagers who are committed to the House and mature in the Word makes every function and ministry effort easier.

Just to take one example, our youth fundraisers are more successful than ever because the mentored youth have caught the vision and are willing to be accountable to help build the youth ministry. They also set the example for the rest of the teens during youth services by entering into praise and worship, taking notes during the message and praying with young people who come forward to give their lives to Christ.

These mentored young men and women are helping our youth pastors "cinch the net" in the youth ministry by making follow-up calls to visitors and making it a personal mission not to lose the teenagers back to the world.

G-MEN is not just about mentoring men. It's about taking over the world with the Gospel. It's about training up the next generation. Young people appreciate the value of mentoring. They're learning life truths before they get into the world and stumble. We're taking followers and making them leaders. We're turning boys into men and young ladies into virtuous women of God.

We now have mentoring groups for women. Every other Wednesday night Rose mentors the wives of the men that I mentor. She has begun by using Dr. Cole's book, *"Communication, Sex & Money"* and they love it. However, the emphasis is on being the help meet for the head and together building their Home Group which builds the church. They invite other women that may be experiencing difficulties to their Home Groups and the relationship heals them.

I believe that anyone can be a leader if they have a mentor to love them and develop them to their full potential in Christ. I believe that anyone can be a leader who loves and develops others to their full potential in Christ. It just takes embracing the process, working the strategy, imparting the anointing, and it all starts *today*.

[1] I Samuel 17:58
[2] John 14:6
[3] Proverbs 23:24

Epilogue

The Lord has instructed me to develop relationships with pastors to help them make the G-MEN strategy a reality in their churches. If you are interested in walking through the process personally to implement this strategy, please contact Mark Glaze at PowerHouse Christian Center in Katy, Texas.

We have a teaching manual and audio tape series that break down the concepts from this book into their simplest components. But, more importantly, I am convinced that the most effective way to grasp these procedures is through *relationship*. Relationships can equip us to accomplish more that we ever could on our own.

I would hate to see anyone's mentoring efforts fail due to a lack of experience or knowledge. We're here to serve and help in any way we can. The Body of Christ is meant to *complete*, not *compete*. "Two are better than one; because they have a good reward for their labour. For if they fall, the one will lift up his fellow: but woe to him that is alone when he falleth; for he hath not another to help him up."[1]

We are pledging to avail ourselves to work with your church to implement this strategy. We will gladly come to your church to walk you through the teaching manual, answer any questions you may have and maintain an ongoing relationship to make sure this strategy accomplishes all that you desire.

We have qualified G-MEN and their wives who would be happy to come in my stead if I were personally unavailable. It is important to me that you have every available resource to ensure success. The men and women from PowerHouse who are actually *in* the G-MEN strategy, are the best source of information and wisdom you will find. The most effective way to grasp and run with a vision is to link up, through relationship, with the visionary.

I strongly suggest that anyone who is ready to move forward with the G-MEN strategy give us a call to talk to us and ask questions. The next step is to visit us at PowerHouse Christian Center and see the G-MEN strategy in operation. The third step might be a pastoral encounter for the G-MEN seminar which is two days w/meals and lodging included.

The pep rally of the 90's is over. The time for *dedication* established us. Now it's time for *implementation*. Call me at 281-391-0095 or email: glazem@powerhousecc.com.

Together we can win!

---

[1] Ecclesiastes 4:9-10

NANCY CORBETT COLE CHARITIES

Nancy Corbett Cole
"The Loveliest Lady in the Land"

A portion of the proceeds from this book will be given to Nancy Corbett Cole Charities, serving the abused, addicted and abandoned. Internationally, "Nancy Corbett Cole Homes of Refuge" provide housing, vocational training and education for abused women and children. In the United States, help is ongoing on an individual and corporate basis.

Nancy Corbett Cole, "The Loveliest Lady in the Land," supported her husband, Edwin Louis Cole, in pursuing his life's mission for 54 years. Behind the scenes, she was a spiritual anchor and provider for many. Before her death in December, 2000, Nancy asked for the assurance that those for whom she had provided would not feel her absence.

To fulfill that end, and for that purpose, Nancy Corbett Cole Charities were established.

By purchasing this book, you have already helped society's under-served and less privileged members. If this book helped you, please consider sending a generous donation as well. Your one-time or continual support will help the helpless, heal the hurting, and relieve the needy. Your gift is fully tax-deductible in the U.S. Send your compassionate contribution to:

Nancy Corbett Cole Charities
P.O. Box 92501
Southlake, TX 76092
USA

Thank you for your cheerful and unselfish care for others.

Watch for more Watercolor Books™

by terrific authors like:

Edwin Louis Cole
Nancy Corbett Cole
G.F. Watkins
Karen Davis
Donald Ostrom

Many more!

www.watercolorbooks.com

For international orders
or publishing, contact
Access Sales International
www.access-sales.com
or
dianae@access-sales.com